SIMPLE SAMPLERS

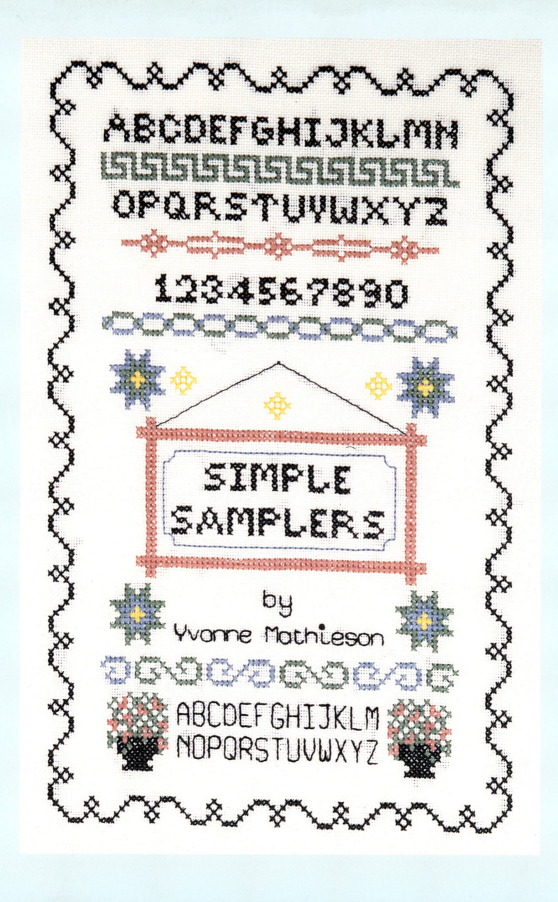

SIMPLE SAMPLERS

YVONNE MATHIESON

B. T. Batsford Ltd, London

ACKNOWLEDGEMENT

I would not have been able to complete this book without help from several sources, and so I would like to thank friends who have seen their gift samplers snatched back for photographing; the patient ladies who have allowed me to use their embroideries and whose names feature by photographs of their work; my father for the loan of the family sampler; and special thanks to my supportive and understanding husband who has taken the photographs and been a sounding board for ideas throughout the whole book process.

First published 1991
© Yvonne Mathieson 1991

All rights reserved. No part of this publication may be reproduced in any form or by any means, without permission from the Publisher.

ISBN 0 7134 6427 5

Typeset by Tradespools Ltd., Frome, Somerset.
And printed in Singapore

For the publishers
B.T. Batsford Limited
4 Fitzhardinge Street
London W1H 0AH

CONTENTS

Author's note 7

Chapter 1 8

Introduction 8; essential information 10; materials and equipment 11; colour 13; the working method 14; getting started 17; sewing techniques 22

Chapter 2 28

Stitching alphabet letters 28; decorative motifs in rows 29; proceeding stage by stage – charting and sewing 33; choosing and displaying mottoes 35

Chapter 3 40

Introducing back stitch alphabets 40; Roman numerals 44; houses 45; working from photographs or pictures 47; other pictorial motifs 51; other stitches 58; working with several colours 59

Chapter 4 62

Borders 62; presentation 73; finishing, mounting and framing 74

Chapter 5 91

Blackwork basics 91; sewing a blackwork sampler 91; using blackwork motifs 95; making blackwork pictures 102

Chapter 6 112

Samplers for gifts 112; designs for greetings cards 117; producing and photographing a card design 123

Further reading 127

Suppliers 127

Index 128

AUTHOR'S NOTE

The intention of this book is that you should use it to help plan and sew your first sampler. Background information is given on fabrics and threads to use as well as on stitch guides, sample alphabets and numbers and suggestions for decorative motifs and borders. The working method is examined in some detail and illustrations are given at each stage of planning and execution.

The sampler shown opposite has been specially worked for this book. If you wish, you can copy this, or you can use it as the basis for the design and sewing of your own ideas.

I hope you will enjoy planning and sewing your sampler as much as I do, and that, once started, you will progress to better and better works.

CHAPTER 1

Introduction

Needleworkers have been producing embroidered samplers for centuries and the works that have survived can provide an interesting reference for present-day sampler sewers. If you wish to go into the history of samplers, there are several excellent examples contained in public collections and museums. The Victoria and Albert Museum in London is a very good place to spend time studying these works from long ago and perhaps gaining an insight into what life then was like. The Fitzwilliam Museum at Cambridge owns a famous collection and odd gems are to be found in local museums and historic houses all over the United Kingdom.

The tradition continues to the present day and although the original purpose and style of samplers has changed, an embroidered sampler is still a very pleasing item to own, and a very satisfying one to create. Samplers were made for various reasons; before books were commonly available they were one very good way of recording stitches and alphabets for future reference. Some samplers showed how stitches were formed by leaving them half done with the needle threaded and inserted to show the next movement.

Fabrics have changed over the years, but generally a sampler seems to have been worked on whatever fabric was available; perhaps a strip left over when some piece of household furnishing or a garment was being made. Stitches have also changed, and while today it is common for samplers to be stitched entirely in cross stitch, samplers from the past show more variety of stitch and sometimes combine counted thread cross stitches with more freely sewn crewel embroidery stitches.

We tend to assume nowadays that the names and dates on the sampler refer to the embroiderer and the date he or she made the sampler. However, we really have no way of knowing, from this distance in time, whether a sampler showing a name and a very young age was actually stitched by the young child, or whether it was made as a present for the child by a doting mother or aunt.

In any case, we cannot but admire the technical skill and hours of painstaking work which must have been put into the making of those beautiful samplers and feel glad that the results of these labours have survived the ravages of time.

Part of the charm of samplers from the past (as well as the present) is that they often contain mistakes. These seem to have been left in on purpose. Perhaps this was to warn the worker to avoid the same mistake in future, but my pet theory is that the mistakes were left in because of the somewhat primitive equipment at the embroiderer's disposal. I should certainly not like to be without my

INTRODUCTION

modern unpicker, and it is a rare person indeed who can finish a sampler without making any mistakes – they do seem to be part of the process. Life is certainly more comfortable for us than it was for our predecessors and we can thank the twentieth century for the blessings of electric light, sharp and effective scissors, needles freely and cheaply available in just the right style and size and an excellent selection of fabrics and threads to suit all purposes.

We have no way of knowing whether or not our own works will survive and what, if anything, our descendants will think about them, but it is certainly good to have in your possession an article created by one of your ancestors. The sampler shown below was worked by Caroline Morse, my father's maternal grandmother, and whilst it is no priceless work of art, it is part of my own

1 Heirloom sampler

INTRODUCTION

family history. It has a small mystery attached to it. Note the date, which reads 1831, and then look at the array of crowns in the centre. Crowns have traditionally been a favourite motif on samplers but there appears to be an anomaly in this particular work – the central crown seems to refer to Queen Victoria, whose coronation did not take place until 1838, seven years later! Add to that the fact that Caroline Morse was not even born at the time, and all the evidence seems to point to the work having been finished in 1881. Did she miss out those two stitches in the date by accident, did they become unravelled later due to carelessness, or was she trying to 'create' an antique? Whatever the truth of the matter, the sampler is an antique now anyway.

If we continue the tradition of sewing samplers today we can take our place with stitchers of the past and enjoy the rewards of this relaxing and soothing pastime. When you pick up your sampler to add a few cross stitches, the pace of life immediately slows and plying the needle has a powerful tranquillizing effect – but, be warned, it can be addictive! Once you get started on your first simple sampler I hope you will find ideas flooding in for new and better works and your eyes will be opened to the design possibilities that exist all around you, if you take the trouble really to look. The increased visual awareness is a reward in itself and by designing your own sampler you can feel you have created a work that is uniquely yours.

Essential information

What is a simple sampler?

The embroidered sampler is a beautiful and durable art form. Samplers began life as reference pieces showing stitches and motifs and were used in the last century as an exercise in stitchcraft for schoolchildren and also to drill them with their alphabets and numbers.

Early embroidered samplers have now become valuable collectors' items and can cost hundreds of pounds. An alphabet sampler is the simplest form, listing A to Z and usually numbers 1 to 10 in different styles and colours. Traditional samplers showed a Biblical text, some of which could be exceedingly gloomy, perhaps reflecting the religious climate of the times. More modern examples often contain a short motto, perhaps the best known being 'home sweet home'. They can also feature pictorial motifs and significant dates, initials, anniversaries, etc.

One way to make a sampler is to buy a kit, where the design and layout work has been done for you, and all materials are provided together with instructions. However, it is not difficult or expensive to design and sew your own personal sampler.

Embroidery is a very relaxing hobby and it is most rewarding to see your own ideas taking shape under the needle. The joy of this particular art form is that mistakes can nowadays be removed painlessly and you are at liberty to change your mind half-way through a piece of work if you wish.

To start sewing the sampler you need two basic items – a chart marked out on graph paper, and a piece of fabric. The first thing to do is to mark out a rectangle on graph paper, then to mark out, using tacking threads, a rectangle on the fabric which corresponds to the graph paper chart. The alphabet is a logical place to start, so choose an alphabet, then mark out the first line of letters on graph paper – one X being equivalent to one cross stitch on the fabric.

It's best to proceed stage by stage, so, having marked out the first line on the chart, sew it on to the fabric using stranded cottons. This line of letters is usually followed by a line of decorative motifs, again chosen and charted and then sewn. As you proceed down the page

INTRODUCTION

and the fabric, your skill and confidence will increase, and there will be time during sewing to think of the next stage and what will look best on the sampler. Mottoes and motifs can be added and also, if you wish, small pictorial representations – perhaps a house, some people, or trees – the choice is yours.

There is no need to worry if your drawing is not too good – even if you cannot draw a straight line, you will be able to sew one using the counted thread method of embroidery. On such a small scale even simple shapes can be very striking and you can use colour to enhance the effect.

A decorative border will finish off the sampler and ensure a good-looking finished article which, when mounted and framed, may turn out to be a family heirloom.

First steps

The best way to start your own sampler is with a pencil and a pad of rough paper – just to give yourself an idea of the shape of your sampler. You don't need to be a great artist – a matchstick man will do very nicely for a person, a few simple lines for a house, and some squiggles for flowers are all you need – you can leave the fine details for later on.

So, will you include an alphabet, numbers, a house, a motto, people, pets, hearts, flowers, dates . . .? As I have said, on a first sampler I think the alphabet is a very good place to start. The letters of the alphabet contain straight lines, diagonals, circles, half circles and many other shapes. Sewing an alphabet is a very good introduction to cross stitch embroidery and will show you the way these shapes can be represented in cross stitch on the fabric. After you have sewn your alphabet and numbers you will have a much better idea of how to tackle the rest of your sampler.

Here is some good news – *you don't have to plan out your whole sampler before you start sewing.*

Materials and equipment

It is not expensive to sew a sampler but there are some essentials. For design work you will need:
- scrap pad for sketching ideas.
- soft pencil (2B)
- size A4 graph paper pad (preferably metric 10 squares to 2cm (13 squares to the inch))
- plastic or rubber eraser for removing mistakes
- ruler
- coloured pencils or felt-tip pens if you wish to plan in colour

For sewing you will need:

Fabric: a piece of evenweave fabric makes an attractive background to the work. The word evenweave means that there are the same number of threads in the fabric horizontally and vertically. This helps with embroidery because we can count these threads and calculate where the stitches will go before we even start to sew.

The fabric I use and recommend is Lanarte. It feels very good to work on and has 10 threads to the centimetre. This approximates to 27 threads to the inch and will result in $13^{1}/_{2}$ stitches to the inch. Colours to use are cream or white and you will need a piece measuring about 40 cm by 50 cm (15 in by 20 in). A list of stockists is given at the back of this book.

If you have problems with your eyes, it is possible you may have trouble seeing the fabric threads, which may cause you difficulty. There are two solutions; the first and best is to buy a needleworker's magnifying glass which loops round the neck and sits on the chest. These are very good and easy to work with once you get used to them. The other solution is to use a different, simpler fabric: I would recommend Aida 14s which is arranged in blocks. One cross stitch fits over one block of the fabric so it is quite easy to see and work

MATERIALS AND EQUIPMENT

with. However, it is not so versatile as the evenweave fabric and although you can produce a very acceptable sampler on it (which is why it is so popular for kits) you will find you cannot make the very fine detailed adjustments which are possible with the greater numbers of threads in the Lanarte evenweave fabric.

If you opt for the Aida fabric, follow the same instructions as for Lanarte but, where we refer to pairs of threads, just use one block of fabric. If you use size 14s your finished sampler will end up almost the same size as on the evenweave fabric; you will have 14 stitches to the inch, as opposed to $13\frac{1}{2}$ stitches to the inch on Lanarte. Ask to see, and feel, both fabrics when you buy, so that you can make an informed decision.

If you choose a fabric with a larger mesh, your finished stitches will be proportionately larger. You could use canvas, but this does mean that you will have to cover the whole piece with stitches, not just the design area. It can be tedious filling in the background, so I would not recommend canvas for this type of sampler.

Needles: you will need blunt ended tapestry needles (size 24–26) with an eye large enough to allow for your sewing thread. Needles should be of a size which will pass through the holes in the weave of your fabric without distortion.

Embroidery scissors: for cutting threads and tidying back of work.

Unpicker: for rectifying any mistakes.

Ordinary cotton sewing thread: for hemming and marking out guide-lines on your fabric.

Stranded cotton threads: six-strand embroidery floss is very useful, available in a wide range of colours, and is not expensive.

Frames: a frame is essential to maintain correct tension. Correct tension is essential for a smooth and tidy finish. The frame is used to keep the fabric taut and make the sewing easier. There are two principal types of frame:

- **Hoops** consist of two wooden rings, one fitting inside the other, with an adjustable screw. There are many sizes suitable from 15 cm (6 in) upwards. The hoop is placed centrally over the area of fabric to be worked and is moved around if the whole design is larger than the hoop (which it usually is). A hoop is suitable for use on evenweave fabric, neat to use, and easily portable. My favourite hoop size is 19 cm ($7\frac{1}{2}$ in) outer diameter.

- **Rectangular frames** are used to keep the entire fabric taut, so the fabric is mounted on this at the beginning of work and not removed until the sampler is finished. A rectangular frame is more often used for heavier fabrics, such as canvas, to avoid the distortion which can happen as work progresses, but you could use a rectangular frame for your sampler. You can buy a frame which has webbing on which to mount your fabric. Cheaper, but just as effective, is a simple picture frame to which you can bind your fabric.

If you wish to spend more money, you can buy a stand for your frame or hoop for even more comfortable working, but this is a luxury and not essential.

Colour

Many traditional samplers were sewn in just one colour – usually black. The use of colour adds another dimension but with a first sampler I think colour should only be used in moderation. There is a practical reason for this. If you sew in one colour only, you will be able to thread the needle and use that thread until it is finished. If you opt for a complicated scheme of colours, you will have to do a lot of work in the planning stage and also much needle threading, starting and finishing off, and re-threading. This will take up a lot of time and slow down your progress. It will also be quite difficult to keep the reverse of the work tidy if there are many threads to sew in.

When you go to the needlework shop and see the marvellous array of colours available it is very easy to be carried away, but I would urge you to practise restraint this first time and bear a few things in mind when buying your stranded cottons:

- The impact will be stronger with just a few colours.
- If using two or three colours, select a colour scheme which is pleasing to you. Bear in mind how the colours react with each other; are they strong, forming a contrast? Or are they harmonious shades of the same colour? If so, beware of getting colours too close together in tone as the difference may not show on the finished work.
- Beware of very light colours. If the fabric is cream or white, a very pale yellow, cream or pink will not show up well against the light background. I love yellow, but have never found it successful in anything but very small amounts. Letters in yellow seem to 'die' against the background and are not at all easy to read.

I like to use a nice strong dark colour for the lettering and numbers and small touches of other colours for decoration and motifs but the choice of colour is a personal one – it's up to you!

The working method

Counted cross stitch on evenweave fabric

In my opinion, this is the simplest and best method for sewing your first sampler.

If you count the threads on the evenweave fabric by laying a ruler across it, you can see there are 20 threads to 2 cm, or 27 threads to one inch. This small mesh makes a good, strong and attractive background to the sampler; if the fabric had a larger mesh, say only fourteen threads to the inch, it would be very loosely woven and sloppy.

When you form the cross stitches you will pass the needle through the holes between the threads. The best way to sew each cross stitch is across two threads of the fabric (both horizontally and vertically). (If we only covered one thread of the background material the stitches would be tiny, very difficult to see and to sew.)

By counting threads you can see that if you work each cross stitch over two threads you will achieve a result of approximately 10 stitches to 2 cm, or $13^{1}/_{2}$ stitches to the inch. Now you know this you can plan out your sampler using graph paper and get an idea of the finished size and scale of the work.

It is best to use graph paper with a scale of 10 squares to 2 cm. If you lay your ruler across the graph paper, you will see that this metric size gives approximately 13 squares to the inch. So, if there are 13 squares to one inch on the graph paper and $13^{1}/_{2}$ stitches to one inch on the fabric, you can see that the chart and finished sewing will be nearly the same size, the sewing being just a little smaller.

If you have a mathematical brain and a taste for absolute precision, you can make a complicated calculation as to the finished size of work, but there is really no need for this. Using chart and fabric which correspond so nearly in size avoids problems and makes planning and design work very simple.

THE WORKING METHOD

Making stitches

One of the joys of sewing samplers is the simplicity of the stitches. When the fabric is mounted in its hoop it will be taut and the stitches should be formed by using a stabbing motion.

You will find the easiest way to form the stitches is to have your most able hand underneath the frame or hoop and your less able hand on top where you can see it. Use short (45 cm or 18 in) lengths of stranded cotton with two strands on the needle and form a cross stitch in four stages as follows:

1. Up from reverse at 1
2. In at 2 (count across over 2 fabric threads, and down over 2 fabric threads)
3. Up from reverse at 3
4. In at 4 to complete cross

As you experiment with this simple cross stitch you will find that it can be worked in many ways to achieve the same result. This will depend on whether you are sewing horizontal, vertical or diagonal lines and the direction in which the stitches are travelling.

It really does not much matter whether you form the stitch starting from top right to bottom left, or vice versa. Just work the stitches in whichever way is more comfortable for you, but please do try to finish with the *top* thread of each cross lying in the same direction. This gives a pleasing even effect, as opposed to a slightly 'jumbled' appearance when care has not been taken to finish off the stitches the same way.

A back stitch will give a neat line and can be used for finely detailed work. It is more versatile than the cross stitch because it can go in any direction you choose. This fine line can be very useful. It is worked in 3 stages:

1. Up from reverse at 1
2. In at 2 (count across 2 fabric threads)
3. Up from reverse at 3, then repeat procedure for next stitch

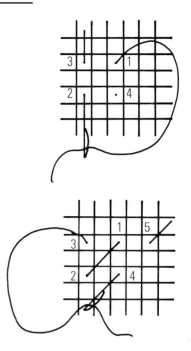

2 Forming a cross stitch over two fabric threads. Up from reverse at 1; in at 2; up from reverse at 3; in at 4 to complete cross; up at 5 ready to start next stitch

3 Finish each stitch in same direction

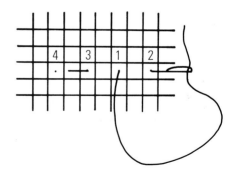

4 Forming a back stitch over two fabric threads (example worked from right to left). Needle up at 1; insert at 2; up again at 3; ready to start next stitch by inserting again at 1 and coming up at 4

THE WORKING METHOD

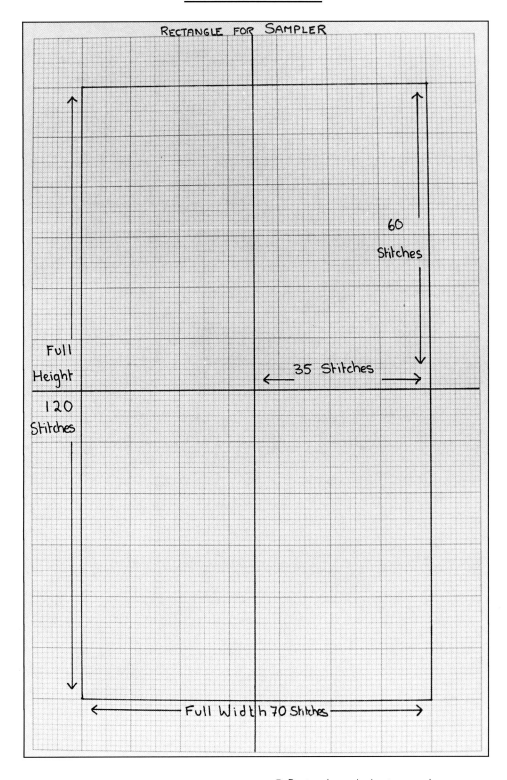

5 Rectangle marked out on graph paper

Getting started

Drawing up the chart

Now is the time to use your A4 graph paper. Each small square on the paper will represent the space taken up by one cross stitch: each x on the chart represents one cross stitch worked over two threads of fabric. The paper has helpful darker lines every ten squares to assist counting.

Mark out a rectangle which will represent the central part of the sampler. Leaving a margin of one large square all around, use a ruler to mark out in pencil on your paper a rectangle covering seven large squares (to represent 70 stitches) across, and twelve large squares (to represent 120 stitches) down. Remember that each small square represents one stitch, worked over two threads (or one block if using Aida fabric).

Now mark out the centre lines across and down. Where these two lines intersect is the *centre* of your chart.

Preparing the fabric

Now that you have a rectangle on the paper, you need to prepare the fabric and mark out a corresponding rectangle on it. First, turn a single hem all round. This is to prevent the edges from fraying (ravelling) during the work. You can use the zigzag on a sewing machine to do this, or sew round by hand, using ordinary cotton thread. You can practise mitring the corners neatly if you wish by turning in the corner and folding over the hem edges.

You could take a short cut and just bind the edges using masking tape; some of my students do this to save time, but it is not my preferred method.

6 Hem or zig-zag fabric edges

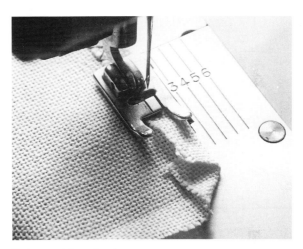

7 Approaching mitred corner

8 Turning mitred corner

GETTING STARTED

Finding and marking the centre point

After hemming, fold the fabric in half from top to bottom and use a contrasting colour of ordinary cotton thread to tack or baste a line of running stitches along the fold to show the centre line.

Don't worry about counting threads at this stage, but *do* be sure to keep the line of stitches along the same line of threads in the fabric.

Open out the fabric again and fold it in half from side to side. Stitch a row of tacking threads along this fold line. Where your two lines of stitches cross is the centre point of your sampler, which corresponds with the centre point on the graph paper.

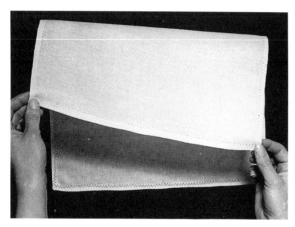

9 Fold fabric top to bottom

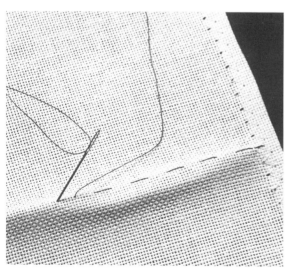

10 Line of tacking threads across

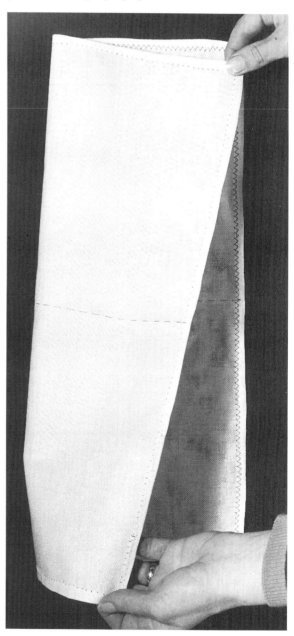

11 Fold fabric side to side

GETTING STARTED

12 Where tacking lines cross is fabric centre point

Marking the rectangle

The next bit will be difficult, but it is worth the trouble of counting threads at this stage to save difficulties later on. You need to mark out the rectangle on your fabric using contrasting cotton thread.

You have already marked out the centre lines horizontally and vertically. Take the horizontal marking line. Start at the centre and work along with the point of your needle, counting *pairs* of threads (remember that each stitch will be worked over two threads). When counting threads, lay the fabric on a dark surface so you can see the pale threads more easily. Thread your needle and use the point to help you count. The full width will be 70 stitches, so if you start from the centre point, you need to count 35 stitches, that is, 35 pairs of threads out from the centre, and mark with a pin.

When you reach this point (35 stitches), sew a marking line up from the horizontal. If you wish, you can make each tacking stitch cover five pairs of threads to help counting. Pull the needle backwards over the first five pairs of threads and make the first tacking stitch, then back under the next five pairs and make the next stitch. Continue until you have covered the required number of pairs of threads. Please don't panic at this stage. It really is the most difficult part of making your sampler and the effort now is well rewarded – it will save lots of work and counting at a later stage.

The full rectangle height is 120 stitches, so starting from the centre line we need to count 60 stitches, i.e. 60 pairs of threads, up from the horizontal centre line. Count these and mark with your tacking thread, then turn left and tack back to the centre.

You have now marked out one quarter of your rectangle; fill in the other three-quarters in the same way and you will have a rectangle tacked out on your fabric which corresponds exactly with the rectangle on the graph paper. The size of the rectangle on Lanarte fabric is approximately 13 × 23 cm (5 × 9 in). This may seem small to you in the centre of a largish piece of fabric, but remember you need to allow spare fabric for a border, and yet more for mounting around card and lacing on the back.

Now heave a sigh of relief that the difficult part is over. This is the framework for your sampler. You are ready to start the chart.

GETTING STARTED

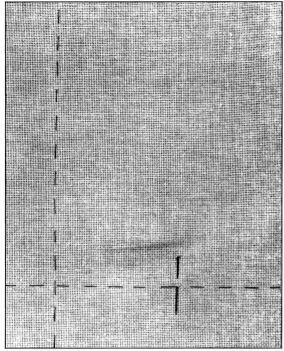

13 Pin marks point 35 pairs of threads out from centre

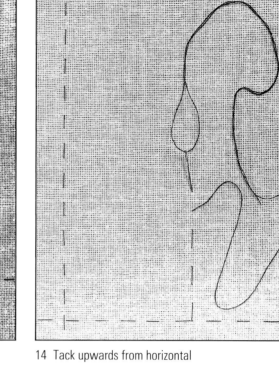

14 Tack upwards from horizontal

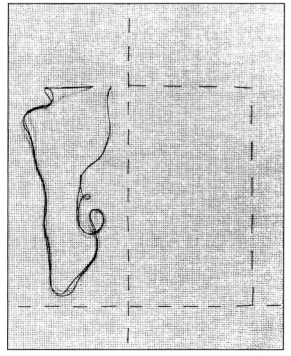

15 Turn left, tack back to centre

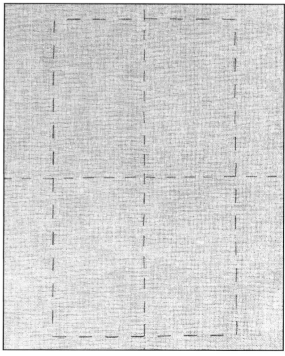

16 Rectangle marked out on fabric corresponds with graph paper rectangle

GETTING STARTED

Making the chart

First, practise a little. Choose a cross stitch alphabet from those shown here and overleaf, and, using a soft pencil, pick out your own initials and mark them in Xs on a spare piece of graph paper. Leave an empty square between letters so that you can read them easily. The large alphabet is more traditional, the smaller alphabet easier to sew.

As an exercise, now put a border of Xs around your initials. Now, counting the Xs, find and mark the central point. This is, in miniature, what you will be doing when designing your sampler layout.

Charting out the alphabet

Select a cross stitch alphabet from the chart given. The chart shown has the same number of squares as the graph paper rectangle you are using. Take a pencil and draw Xs on your graph paper to chart out your first line of letters. Leave a blank square between letters.

Centring the alphabet

The alphabet will look best balanced nicely between left and right. When you chart out the line of letters you may have two or three spaces left blank at the right-hand edge. You can either leave it like this, *or*, if you wish to centre the work, you can make the minor adjustment by starting to sew your cross stitches one or two spaces in from the marking line on your fabric.

In the example overleaf the alphabet starts one square in from the edge.

17 Chart of large alphabet and numbers

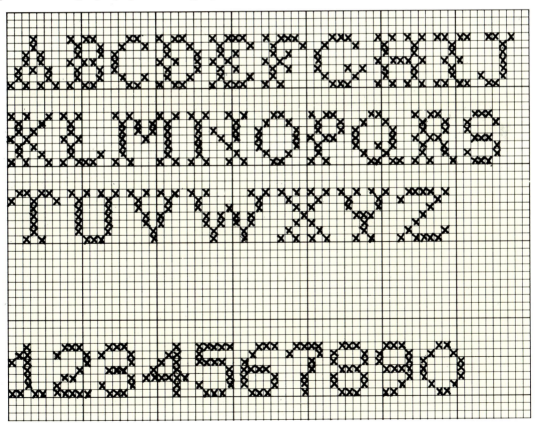

SEWING TECHNIQUES

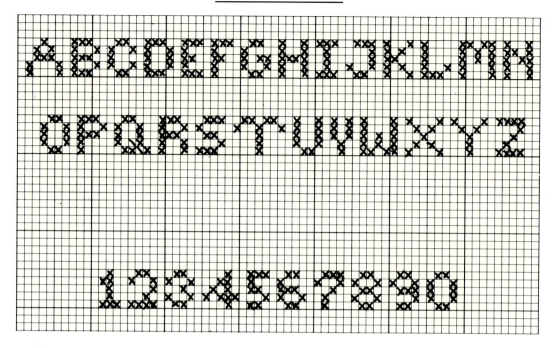

18 Chart of small alphabet and numbers

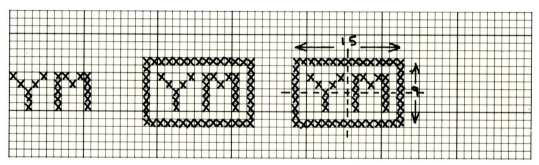

Sewing techniques

Now you have charted your first line of letters, you are ready to sew this on your fabric.

19 Charting exercise with your own initials. Copy out your own initials; put a border round; count squares and find and mark centre point

Posture and lighting

You will enjoy sewing your sampler if you are comfortable and can see to work easily. Good lighting is very important, and if you are right-handed, a strong light source coming over your left shoulder is ideal. (For left-handers, the light should come from the right.) If I cannot work in daylight I like to use an anglepoise lamp, which throws a concentrated beam of light and makes the fabric threads easy to see. If your eyesight needs assistance, a magnifier which hangs round the neck can be very useful.

If you sit in an armchair to sew you could easily get an aching neck from leaning over your work. To avoid this I like to have a cushion on my knees and rest the work on this. Alternatively you could work at a table or desk and rest your wrist on this.

SEWING TECHNIQUES

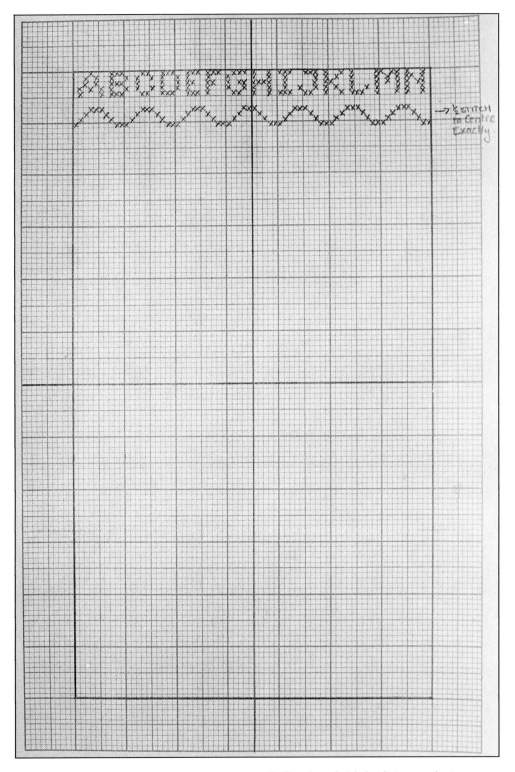

20 First line of alphabet letters on chart

SEWING TECHNIQUES

Using the hoop

Take your embroidery hoop and tighten the screw adjuster so the smaller hoop fits snugly inside the larger one. Now loosen off the screw just a little (about two turns).

Lay your fabric out smoothly right-side upwards on a flat surface. Now slide the smaller hoop underneath the fabric in the appropriate place for you to begin sewing. Take the larger wooden hoop and press it down firmly over the fabric and the smaller hoop, making sure the fabric is tight as a drum. Then, using a screwdriver, tighten the adjustable screw to hold everything firm.

It is very important to have the fabric taut because this will give a correct tension and make for a neat finish to your sewing.

21 Make yourself comfortable and work in a good light
22 Placing hoop on fabric

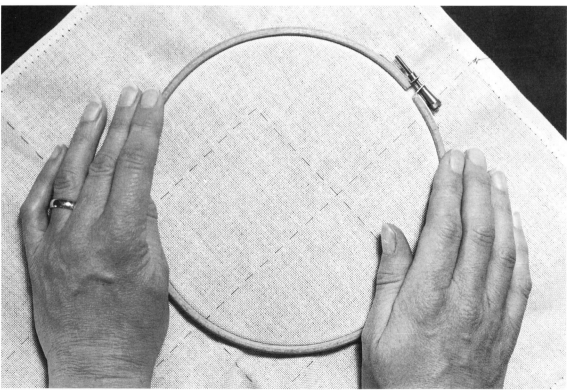

SEWING TECHNIQUES

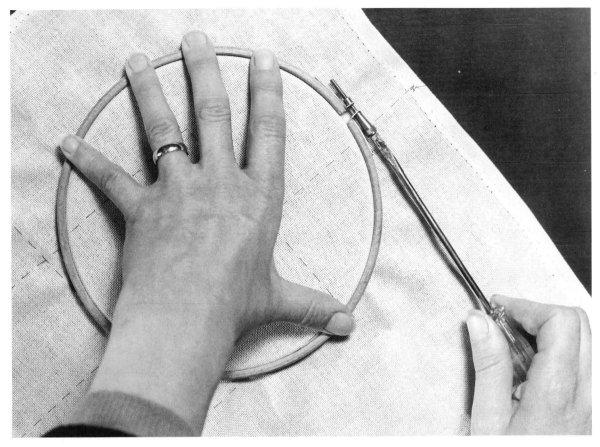

23 Tighten with screwdriver to hold fabric taut

Threading the needle

Pull out and cut off a length of approximately 45 cm (18 in) of stranded cotton thread.

Separate two strands from the six-stranded cotton as shown over the page.

To thread the needle you can simply moisten the ends to stiffen them, then pass them through the eye of the needle. You can use a needle threader if you wish.

Starting and finishing

Before you take the plunge and sew your first stitch, here are a few pointers on general techniques.

Having threaded your needle, it is not a good idea to put a large knot at the other end. This would make for a bumpy sampler and if the knot unravels it can cause you problems later on. The best way to start off sewing is as follows:

From the right side (the top), insert the needle at random about an inch from where you wish to begin your first stitch. Then, bring the needle up from the reverse in the correct place and sew your first stitch, still leaving the loose end on the right side of fabric. After you have sewn three or four cross stitches, finish a stitch with the needle at the reverse of fabric, turn over the work to the wrong side, then pull through the loose end and oversew it neatly to the back of work. Then snip off any loose end to avoid it tangling with the working thread. This way of starting off gives a fairly smooth finish to the work.

SEWING TECHNIQUES

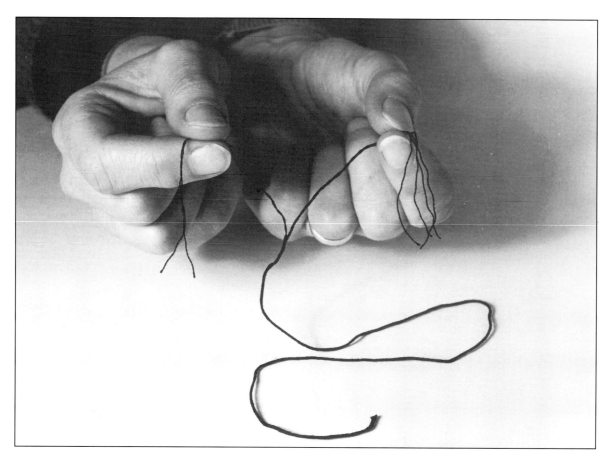

24 Separate two strands

To finish off, when you are nearly at the end of a length of thread, turn over the work and oversew the thread neatly into the back of the stitches. Then, using small embroidery scissors, snip the end off carefully and neatly.

Mistakes

If you make a mistake and notice it immediately, just unthread the needle and unpick carefully using your needle or an unpicker. You can then correct as you go along. Early sampler sewers used to leave mistakes in their work. Perhaps they did not have such good unpickers as we do, or perhaps they left the mistakes in to warn them against repeating them.

If you need to correct a mistake that happened some time back, the best way is to cut the stitches from the right side, being really careful not to damage the fabric, and then remove loose ends from the wrong side. Finally, insert the correct stitches, using a fresh length of thread.

If you find yourself doing a lot of unpicking, don't hesitate to discard the thread and use a new length, because the thread can get 'tired' from too much handling and could start to look a little fuzzy and uneven.

A word of warning here: please do not be tempted to carry the thread long distances across the back of work, especially where there will be no stitching on the front. The thread will show through from the back and may spoil the appearance of your sampler.

SEWING TECHNIQUES

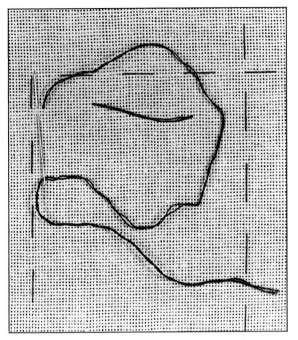

25 Start of sewing with loose end left on right side

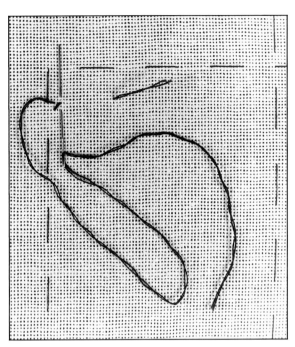

26 First cross stitch completed, ready for next

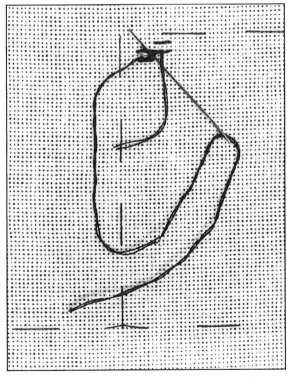

27 Pull through loose end and oversew to reverse of work

CHAPTER 2

Stitching alphabet letters

Sewing your first letters

Having read the suggestions on sewing techniques, you are now ready to sew your first A. The fabric should be mounted on the hoop, the needle threaded with two strands of thread and the chart ready at hand.

Look at the top left-hand corner of your guide threads and count down and in to where you should put the bottom left-hand cross stitch of the A. Sew your first cross stitch and then put in the second, carefully following the Xs on the chart. Where stitches butt up together, use the same holes of fabric for the top of one stitch and the bottom of the next.

Following the chart, finish off sewing the A and then look back to see what you have done. Now start on the B, remembering to leave a space between the two letters.

Complete the first row of letters in the same way. As you sew, you will find it is much easier, where possible, to bring the needle up from reverse in an 'empty' hole rather than

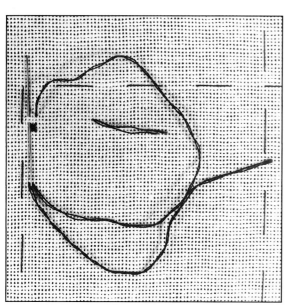

28a First cross stitch complete, place second stitch on top

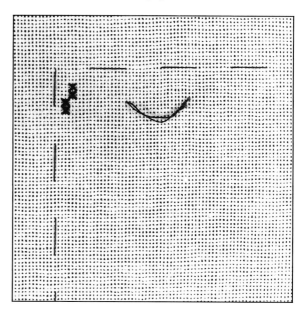

28b Four stitches completed, loose end still on surface, ready to be oversewn into back

DECORATIVE MOTIFS IN ROWS

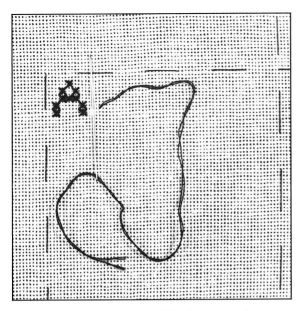

28c A completed, start sewing B leaving a space between letters

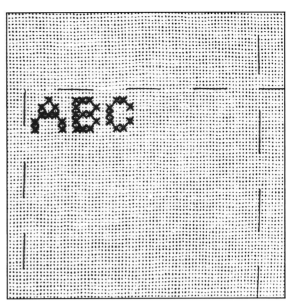

28d First three letters completed

one which already contains a stitch, where snagging could occur. Form the stitches whichever way is easiest, always remembering to finish off the cross stitch with top thread lying in the same direction as the other stitches. After this, you will need a rest from sewing so now is the time to plan your first row of decoration.

Decorative motifs in rows

Traditional 'band' samplers were long narrow strips of fabric which featured horizontal rows of patterns, and this is the style I like to use for a simple sampler. The narrow width means that you never sew any one pattern for long enough to get tired of it and the rows of patterns, or decoration, allow plenty of opportunity for experiment with both shape and colour. The small size of this simple sampler means that very large and complicated motifs will look out of place in these bands of decoration and perhaps they are better saved for use in future, more ambitious, works.

I like to introduce my second and third colours in these rows of decoration which separate the rows of letters and numbers. Now is the time to get out the coloured pens or pencils and spare graph paper and doodle around to see if you can design a repeating motif. The world around you is full of ideas; carpets, wallpaper, magazines and advertisements are all good hunting grounds for motifs, and if you keep a scrap book you will soon find you have plenty of source material. To get you started I have charted some simple suggestions overleaf (X represents one colour, and O a contrasting colour), but of course it is much more rewarding if you invent your own.

DECORATIVE MOTIFS IN ROWS

29 Decorative bands charted in rows for width of 70 stitches.
X = first colour; O = second colour

DECORATIVE MOTIFS IN ROWS

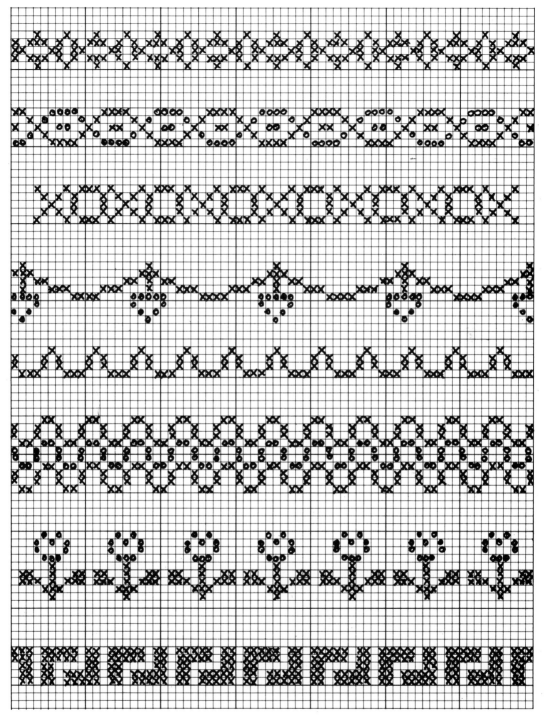

30 More decorative bands charted

DECORATIVE MOTIFS IN ROWS

CHARTING AND SEWING

Proceeding stage by stage – charting and sewing

These rows are fun to chart out and it is interesting to see how the contrasting colours react with each other. When you have decided on your pattern, add it to your master chart. To avoid a cramped effect, leave a good vertical space between rows; I would suggest a minimum of two squares on the chart.

Centring the work accurately

For a balanced appearance it is best to centre the work as accurately as possible.

If your decorative motif contains an odd number of stitches, you will find that the evenweave fabric is more versatile and that fine adjustments can be made. For example, the top line of decorative motifs (under letters A–N) is formed from groups of three cross stitches. Starting at the centre, you can straddle the centre stitch over the central tacking line, thus centring the work very precisely. This is easier to sew than to draw on the chart. When you make your chart, just make a small note to make the half-stitch shift when you come to sew.

If you are using Aida fabric you will not be able to straddle your cross stitch over the centre line, as the fabric construction will prevent this. You need to decide which will be your 'centre' stitch (either to the right or the left of the centre line) and stick to that decision throughout the sampler. The alternative is always to use a motif containing an even number of stitches, but you may find this cramps your creative style.

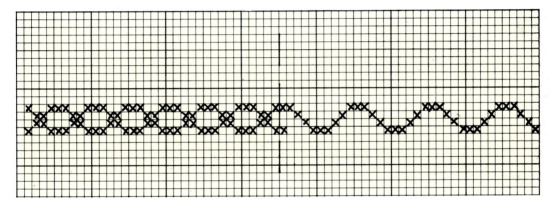

31 Pattern used on sampler – make note to centre exactly when sewing by straddling centre stitch over tacked centre line

If your decorative motif contains an even number of stitches, start sewing at the central guide-line and butt the cross stitches up to this, working out first to the left, and then to the right. The same procedure applies for evenweave or Aida fabric.

I like to complete the whole row with one colour first, then add the second colour and watch the different effect being created under the needle. Colours sometimes react together in quite unexpected ways.

After the first decorative band you can add your second row of alphabet letters to the master chart and sew them. You could centre this line, or just sew it and add a small motif

A worked example of some decorative bands of pattern. Four colours have been used in different combinations. French knots are included for texture, and a plain four-colour border, which needs no counting, has been added

CHARTING AND SEWING

32 First two lines of letters with two lines of decoration

after the Z just to balance things up a bit. Now you have the idea, you can continue down your sampler, charting first and then sewing, putting in another row of decoration and then some numbers.

Feel free to experiment – after all, that's what samplers are for. Use your spare graph paper for doodles and ideas and try to think what else you will include on your sampler to make it distinctly yours. There is plenty of time to think while you are sewing and it is hoped that some good ideas will start coming to you.

Choosing and displaying mottoes

Choosing a motto

It's time to start thinking about a motto. The motto or proverb you choose will affect the character of your sampler. If it is very short, perhaps three or four words, you will be able to set it out in large letters and perhaps display it within a border to give it prominence. If it is longer, you will need to use a smaller alphabet to fit it all on and set it out tidily. If it has three or four lines of words, you will have to decide whether to start it at the left-hand edge, or to centre each line across the fabric.

Whatever you choose, you will need to experiment with your pencil and graph paper to achieve a pleasing layout. When you have made your preliminary sketches, consider how and where they will fit on your sampler. The motto can go anywhere on your sampler, near the top, centre or bottom, or even around the outside, but perhaps for a first sampler, a very short, simple motto will suffice. I used the best known, 'home sweet home.'

Displaying the motto

I doodled around with the three words, 'home sweet home', until I had what I felt was a symmetrical layout. I charted out the three words on spare graph paper, and counted how many squares they occupied. Then I centred the design on the master chart, working out from the centre.

To make the motto stand out from the rest of the sampler I added a border, outlined in back stitch and filled in with a small motif. I felt there were gaps at either side of the first 'home', so put in the hearts at either side, balancing up the colours. You can see on the chart that there are four vertical squares between the two lines of words. When I added the crosses below the first 'home' I centred this line vertically, by shifting down half a stitch to leave an equal space top and bottom.

Displaying the motto gives opportunities for creating a very pleasing effect, so be prepared to take a bit of time over this stage, to get it right.

CHOOSING AND DISPLAYING MOTTOES

33 Chart for *Home Sweet Home* motto

Motto and border stitched

CHOOSING AND DISPLAYING MOTTOES

More about mottoes

More complicated sentiments can form the basis of future works. Many people have a favourite proverb, saying or verse. One way to find a good one for a sampler is to get together with a group of friends and have a brainstorming session. You will be surprised at how many apt sayings you know.

You could also use reference books or books of quotations in your local library. These are often quite weighty tomes, so go prepared to spend some time in the reference section, armed with pen and paper for taking notes. You could also cast your mind back to childhood days which seem, from an ever-increasing distance, to be peppered with admonishments and reminders.

Here are a few themes and suggestions to get you started:

Home sweet home
East, west – home's best
Home is where the heart is
Home is where the hearth is (I used this for a firescreen)
Love builds a happy home
Bless this house
Bless this (mortgaged) house
Bless this (very heavily mortgaged) house

Friendship is . . .
A true friend is a gift of God
The way to a friend's house is never long

Time and tide wait for no man
Procrastination is the thief of time
Never put off till tomorrow what you can do today
Never do today what you can put off till tomorrow
Time – the great healer
A stitch in time saves nine

March winds and April showers, bring forth May flowers

Whether the weather be fine, or whether the weather be not,
We have to weather the weather, whether we like it or not.

Do as you would be done by, be done by as you did
Many hands make light work
Merry nights make sad mornings

34 Chart for *Bless this House*

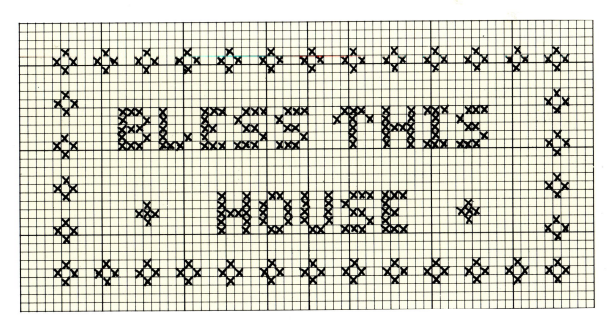

CHOOSING AND DISPLAYING MOTTOES

Life is what happens to you while you're busy making other plans

It's nice to be important, but it's important to be nice

The love of money is the root of all evil

All that glisters is not gold

As this is not a reference book of quotations I shall not go on, but you can see there is a wealth of material to choose from. You can make a motto or verse part of an alphabet sampler or the subject of a separate sampler, where you can give it more prominence. You can spend a very pleasant few hours deciding which sentiment you will 'immortalize' on your sampler and how you will choose to display it.

35 Chart for *Don't dream it – be it*

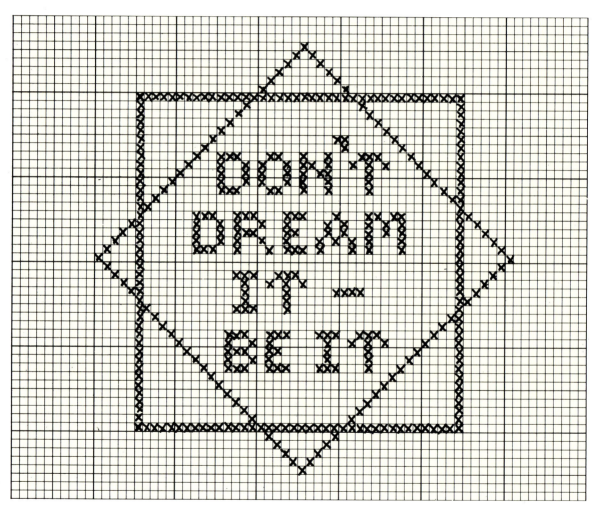

CHOOSING AND DISPLAYING MOTTOES

CHAPTER 3

The first part of the Home Sweet Home sampler we are making uses cross stitch only, but you can see that on the border around the motto I have used back stitch to achieve a fine line.

Cross stitches are very attractive but have the disadvantage that, on such a small scale as this, it is not easy to show fine details. The back stitch, however, is much more versatile and can be used to gain an effect similar to a pen and ink line. Back stitch is simple to work and is shown in the stitch diagram in fig 4. You can achieve a fine line by using two threads of stranded cotton on the needle, or an even finer line using just a single thread.

If you wish to put a house on your sampler you will be able to get a much more detailed effect using back stitches, as you can see from the charted designs of houses later in this chapter.

Introducing back stitch alphabets

On the sampler overleaf I have included a back stitch alphabet as a way to get used to sewing with this different stitch. If you work this alphabet you will see how versatile it can be.

Working a back stitch over a single thread

Until now we have been sewing each stitch over two threads of the evenweave fabric. If you sew the back stitch alphabet like this it will appear somewhat jagged and angular (fig 36). If you wish to achieve a curve, you can slip in a small extra back stitch over just a single thread of fabric and adjust the stitch at either side (fig 37). That may sound a little confusing, so let's take the letter B as an example. Here one square represents a single thread of fabric (fig 38).

When you sew the letter V you have a choice of methods. I prefer to make each back stitch double length (over four horizontal threads) but across only one vertical thread, to make the letter look more natural and still fit into the space available.

This is the main reason I prefer to use evenweave, rather than Aida fabric. The Aida is, admittedly, easier to see, but is less flexible, as it does not easily allow these refinements to be made. If you are using evenweave fabric you will probably have found by now that your eyes have adjusted to it and that the fabric threads are easier to see than when you started sewing.

When you are sewing small stitches you will need to maintain an even and tight tension on your hoop to avoid the tiny stitches slipping to the back and disappearing.

If you enjoy sewing with backstitch, you will find more possibilities opening up for you. You can use the fine line to go in any direction and vary the stitch length and, with a bit of

INTRODUCING BACK STITCH ALPHABETS

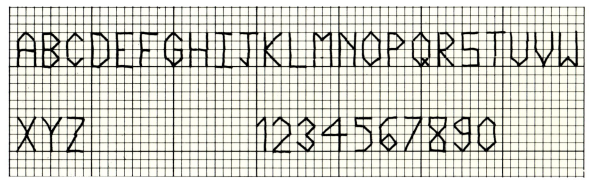

36 Angular back stitch alphabet and numbers with each stitch over two fabric threads

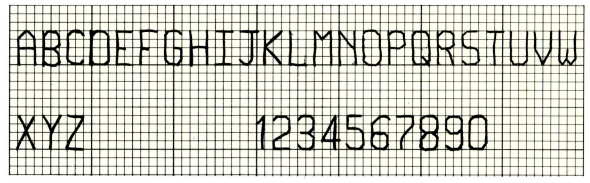

37 Rounded back stitch alphabet and numbers using half stitches over single fabric thread at curves

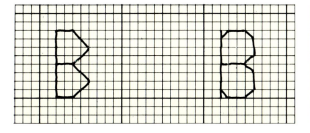 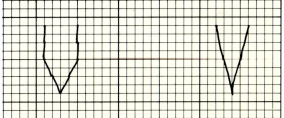

Jagged back stitches each worked over two threads

Use of half stitch over a single thread to round off corners

Stitches over two horizontal threads but across one vertical thread down towards point

Long stitches over four horizontal threads but across one vertical thread to form pointed shape

38 Letter B enlarged. 1 square = 1 fabric thread

39 Two ways of forming letter V enlarged

INTRODUCING BACK STITCH ALPHABETS

practice, you will find that you can represent images and fine details which are just not possible at this small scale when using a cross stitch.

Sewing the back stitch alphabet will show you how to make a small circle, and how to achieve a curve. If you progress to the lower-case alphabet you will find you are almost writing freehand, but using needle and thread instead of a pen. You could also further reduce the letter width on the lower-case alphabet by making the letters one and half stitches wide. As the alphabets reduce in size, it becomes harder to mark them out on graph paper, so perhaps a few experiments on the edge of your fabric would be a valuable exercise. I enjoy the challenge of working in miniature and seeing just how small you can make the letters before they become illegible. Please do practise anything adventurous on the edge of fabric (it will eventually be hidden in the frame) before committing yourself to something difficult on the actual sampler. Mistakes at this small scale can be easily made, but not so easily removed.

Another, and closely related, type of embroidery is blackwork embroidery, which uses double running stitch or back stitch. I have used blackwork quite a bit myself in samplers, and have therefore included a separate chapter on the subject.

Bless this House sampler opposite uses back stitch extensively, for alphabets and bands of decoration. The motto and pictorial motifs are afterthoughts

40 *Conscience* sampler uses back stitch for the grandfather clocks and nagging reminders in the motto

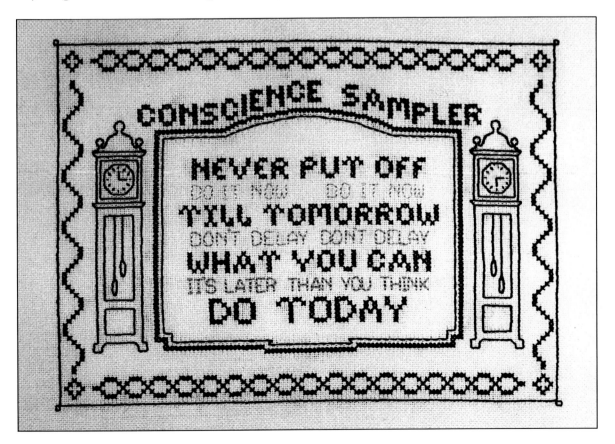

ROMAN NUMERALS

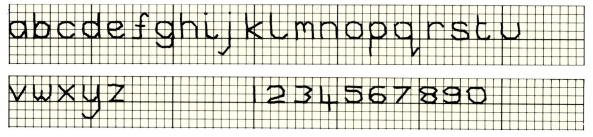

41 Lower case alphabet and numbers

Roman numerals

Sewing the Roman numerals

I am fascinated by Roman numerals, although I must confess I find difficulty in remembering them, so they are a good feature to put on a sampler. You can sew them in the same way as the back stitch alphabet. You could even put on the year worked out in Roman numerals. I have included some key figures to help you. You can check the Roman numerals for the current year by looking at the credits at the end of television programmes; these are often

42 Alphabet in small capitals

shown in this way. Make sure the programme is not a repeat from a previous year!

The chart and sampler are progressing nicely now, and by this time you should be feeling fairly comfortable with the ideas of sketching, charting out and sewing. Now, it's time to have a bit of fun working out the freest and most creative part of the sampler, the pictorial section.

43 Roman numerals

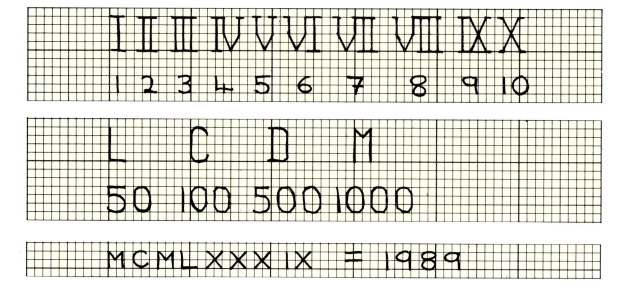

Houses

Houses

If you live in a nice house and want to portray this on your sampler you could chart it out from a photograph. Separate instructions for this are shown later in this chapter. If you don't want to show your own house, you could design and chart out your dream home, or you could base your design on the small houses shown here. Remember to simplify the lines and keep them basic, and try not to be too ambitious on this, your first sampler.

44 Houses – cross stitch only or cross and back stitch combined. Use colours to enhance the effect. Experiment with small back stitches using single thread to achieve very fine details

It could be that you will see in a cross stitch magazine or design source book a house already charted out that you would like to use on your sampler. If it is small, use it by all means, but you will need to check on the size of graph paper used for the design and compare it with your own. Often the best and most appealing designs turn out to be much bigger than they appear at first sight, which is how they are able to include all that attractive detail in the first place. They can also use several colours, which might slow down and complicate the sewing process for a beginner. Before you commit yourself to sewing, check that your chosen design will be in proportion and appropriate to the rest of your sampler; if not, perhaps it is better to paste that clever design into your scrapbook for the future.

HOUSES

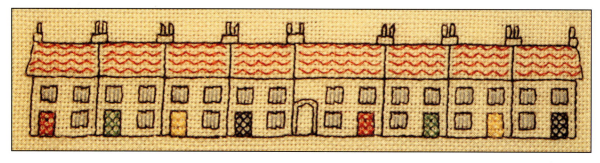

Small terraced houses

Large terraced houses

Semi-detached houses

Detached houses

WORKING FROM PHOTOGRAPHS OR PICTURES

Detached cottages

As you can see, the joy about working on this small scale is that you don't need to be a great artist to portray a house, and the guidelines on the graph paper grid are a help with straight lines.

I find it simplest to start with a central part of a design; on a house I start charting at the front door. I put that on the chart using Xs for cross stitch, or lines for back stitch, then radiate out in all directions adding porches and windows and trying to keep reasonably symmetrical. Then I finish with the walls and roof, usually adding a chimney or two.

Don't worry if your straight lines are a bit wobbly on the chart; if the fabric is taut in the hoop when you sew, the lines will turn out beautifully straight. This is one area where I think embroidery scores over drawing and painting: the grid is a valuable guide-line and any mistake can be quickly and simply removed and corrected.

Working from photographs or pictures

We are surrounded by pictures of houses – for example, there is usually a good selection of houses of all shapes and sizes in the property pages in the local newspaper.

Alternatively you may wish to chart out a design direct from a photograph. The choice of photograph is important; choose one that is about the right size if at all possible. If this is not possible you will be able to enlarge or reduce the design – see instructions in fig 60 for squaring up or down.

Remember your work is based on a square grid which could present a problem if your subject was not photographed square on. If

45 Base line of simple sampler; use coloured pencils for planning

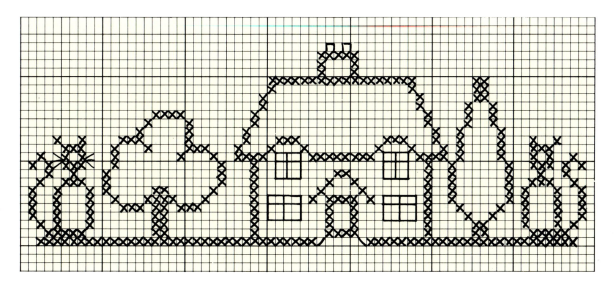

WORKING FROM PHOTOGRAPHS OR PICTURES

you point the camera upwards at a house, the roof will appear foreshortened in the photograph, and so will look too small if you trace it and sew it as it is. If your subject is photographed at an angle, you will find it more difficult to translate the shapes and lines into stitches which will fit easily on to this evenweave fabric.

Personally I feel that a small house shown on a sampler, especially one as small as your simple sampler, should be kept very basic, and I like the 'primitive' effect of a few lines and stitches. The house becomes more of a sketch or impression than a factual reproduction.

Finished base line of sampler

Tracing designs from photographs or pictures in magazines etc.

Select a design containing strong simple lines which are suitable for translation on to a grid form. Remember that a simple design will be most effective and that much of the detail in a photograph will be lost.

1. Pin or clip tracing paper (kitchen greaseproof will do) over the photograph or picture. Using a 2B pencil, trace the simple lines of the picture. Bear in mind that you will be sewing this picture, and simplify it as much as possible.

2. Remove the tracing paper, turn over, and shade on the reverse of traced lines using a soft pencil.

3. Pin the tracing, correct way round, over graph paper.

4. Pencil over the lines of the design.

5. Remove the tracing paper and look at the design on the graph paper. (You could short-cut stages 2–5 by using tracing graph paper.)

6. See where and if the design lines coincide with the grid lines on the graph paper. Remember that each small square represents two threads of fabric.

7. Decide whether to use cross stitches or back stitches, or a combination. If using cross stitches, you will have to stick exactly to the squares on the graph paper. If using back stitches you can work more freely, varying the number of threads and the direction of the stitches. For example, to portray a gradual slope on a roof you could use a back stitch covering three vertical fabric threads but only one horizontal fabric thread.

8. If you are confident, start to sew. If you are not yet sure, sketch out the design again underneath the tracing, adapting the design to fit the grid, until you are sure you know how you will place the stitches.

Enlarging or reducing the size of a design

Personally, I have never felt the need to enlarge or reduce a design to use on a simple sampler; I prefer to hunt around for something that is the right size in the first place, or merely to doodle in pencil until I achieve a design I like. However, for other forms of embroidery you are almost certain to need, at some stage, to change the size of a design, which is why I include the topic here.

There are a number of ways to tackle this task. In this age of technological marvels there are machines which are a great help. There may be a photocopy shop or a printing firm nearby that can enlarge or reduce a picture size. They may also be able to translate a photograph into a line drawing and so make tracing more simple. Whenever I visit a printer I am always amazed at the things their machines and computers can do, and new developments are taking place all the time. It's worthwhile having a word with printers to see how they can help, and, in any case, their workshops are usually interesting places which may themselves give you some new ideas.

If you wish to be independent and to enlarge a design at home, you will have to resort to the tried and tested method known as 'squaring up'. If you have not used this method before I suggest that, before you tackle anything important or complicated, you look at the example and then work through a small experimental exercise on your own, just to get the idea of the method. You will see that the example given contains both straight and curved lines and, for simplicity, the grid has been doubled in size. Here are general instructions for squaring up:

1. Study the examples given. Choose a small design yourself for enlargement and draw or trace on to graph paper. I suggest something very simple, containing straight and curved lines.

2. Rule a box round the design and mark off equal squares on a grid. As you are using graph paper it's sensible to use the bold lines on the paper.

3. Number the letters and squares on the grid – remember map references at school?

4. Decide by how much you wish to increase the design size. The given examples were doubled in size.

5. On a new sheet of graph paper, draw up a new grid with each square double the original size. Number up the grid to correspond with the original.

6. Referring to the small original grid, compare the two, and put small pencil marks on the new grid where design lines intersect with grid lines. Use the letters and numbers so you don't lose your place, and remember that the straight lines will take up double the number of squares now.

7. When you have enough marks you can do a 'join the dots' exercise. You should find the original design emerging at its new size.

WORKING FROM PHOTOGRAPHS OR PICTURES

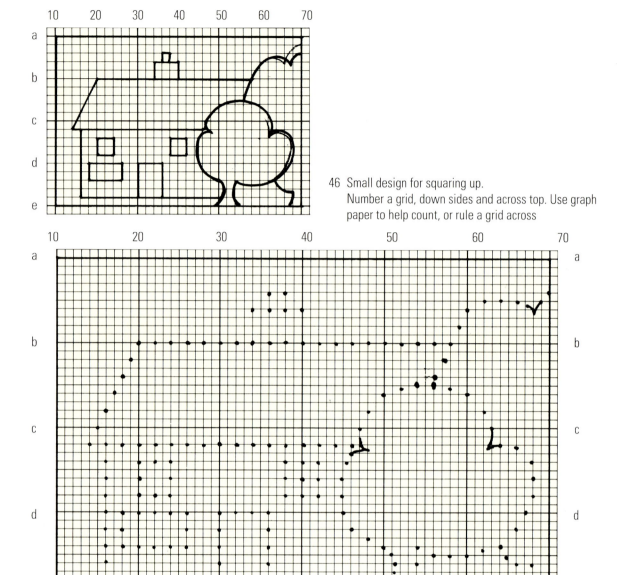

46 Small design for squaring up.
    Number a grid, down sides and across top. Use graph paper to help count, or rule a grid across

47 Grid enlarged (in this case, doubled) and marked out with dots.
    1. Rule a new grid in the bigger size – number the squares as before on the new scale
    2. Pencil on dots where the lines of the design on the small diagram coincide with the grid intersections – e.g. at B30 and D30

OTHER PICTORIAL MOTIFS

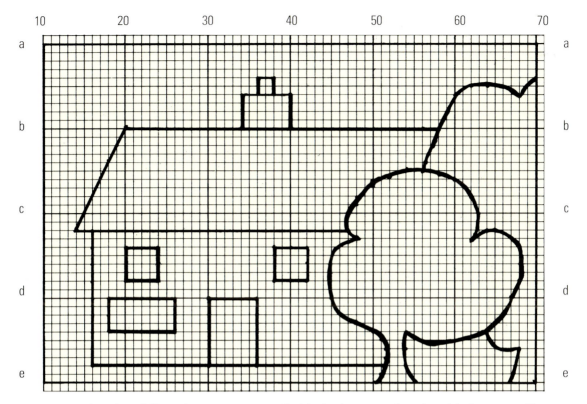

48 Join the dots to see the enlarged design emerge. You could now add more detail. To reduce a design size, reverse the whole process

To reduce a design size, follow the same principles but work the exercise backwards to reach a small new design.

The example used was merely doubled; if you want to change size by a different proportion you will need to calculate the new grid size accordingly. You may find it more convenient not to use the graph paper in this case, but to measure out your grid on plain paper.

You may find that changing the design size results in its looking a bit different – for example, with an enlarged design there will be more opportunity to add detail, so you could start to add some now. If reducing a design in size you may lose details from the original. It is important to bear these facts in mind when selecting designs for this treatment and this is one area where experimentation can be particularly valuable.

Other pictorial motifs

After the house there is still some space to fill. You can include things important to you – significant dates or initials, people, pets, flowers, hearts, trees etc. You could use the original sampler colours or branch out into glorious technicolour. This is a good time to experiment with coloured pens or pencils on graph paper.

Do not worry if you are not a great artist. At this small scale it is enough to suggest a shape and colour, without worrying too much about detail or realism. Objects with straight lines and simple angles lend themselves well to translation into cross stitch, whereas intricate floral designs with flowing curves will be very

OTHER PICTORIAL MOTIFS

difficult to portray in the space you have available.

I have charted some doodles here to get you started. I have shown outlines only for the hearts and trees but of course you can fill them in with one colour, or several colours, if you wish. I think hearts can look really good filled in with several shades of pink; just work inwards making sure you follow the outline each time.

If you are artistic you should be able to chart out your own motifs without difficulty. Children's books, with their clean lines and bold primary colours, can be a very useful design source. If you do not like the idea of designing motifs yourself, there are many books and magazines available with designs ready charted out for you to copy. Colour choices will also be suggested, or you can make your own. Your craft shop should carry a good selection. However, as with house designs, you will need to check that a charted-out design will be in proportion with your own sampler. The grid on which it is printed may well be a different size from your own chart, so it is worthwhile doing a bit of checking before you reach for the needle and thread. If it is a complicated design, you don't need to copy it out laboriously, but you will need to count how many squares it occupies and translate this into your own chart size.

49 Hearts in varying sizes

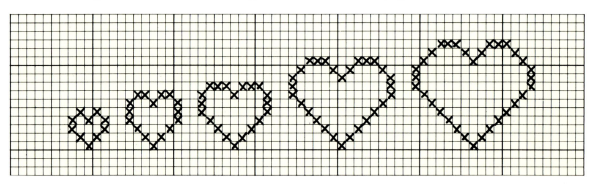

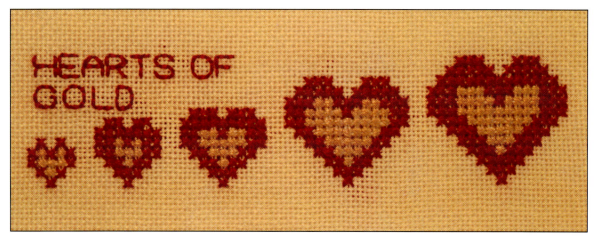

OTHER PICTORIAL MOTIFS

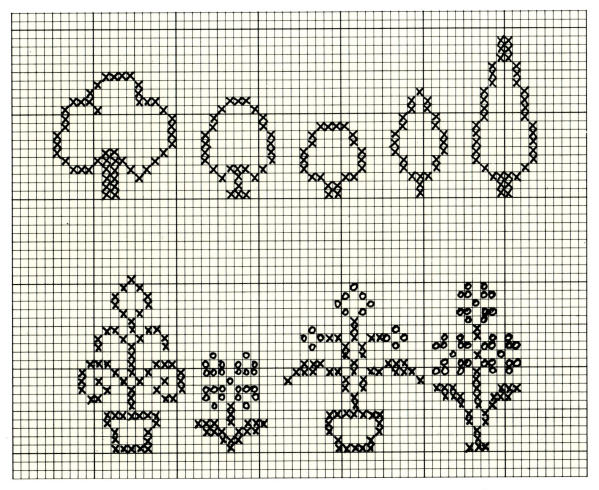

50 Trees and flowers; plan to use colour

Experiment with stitch variations and mixing colours on the needle

OTHER PICTORIAL MOTIFS

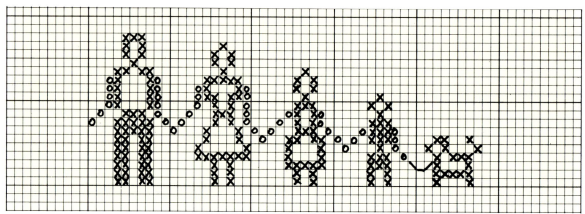

51 Standing people

OTHER PICTORIAL MOTIFS

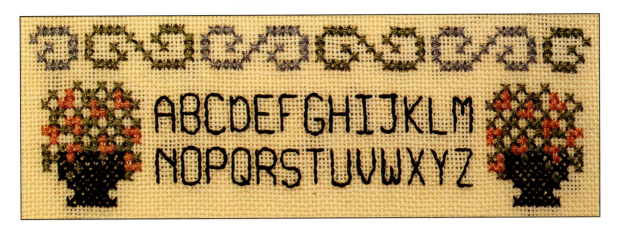

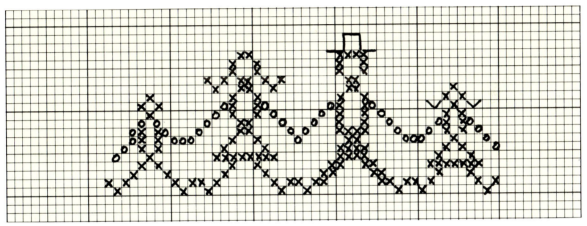

52 Dancing people

OTHER PICTORIAL MOTIFS

Experiment with different stitches and styles

You can use a cut and paste technique to help here. One way of doing this is to count and mark the rough outline of your chosen design on to a piece of spare graph paper. You could also suggest colours at this stage with a few scribbles with coloured pens or pencils. Then cut round the outline and experiment by placing it in different positions on your own sampler. You will then be able to see if it is in proportion, whether it is appropriate to the rest of the work, and where it will look best. If all is well, you can then stick the paper outline to your chart (I use solid stick adhesive, no mess, no fuss), and when you come to sew you can follow the exact cross stitch details directly from the book where you first saw the design.

Perspective and true-to-life proportions are two things which need not concern us. I think part of the charm of samplers is their primitive treatment and complete lack of consideration of size or scale, especially in the selection and placing of these free little motifs – spot motifs, as they are called. It is certainly not unusual to see a standing figure or animal which quite obviously could never fit inside the house, and if the flying birds shown on old samplers are shown to scale they must all have belonged to the vulture family!

Your sampler will benefit from some symmetry and it is common to see these spot motifs featuring as mirror images on either side of a sampler. Of course, anomalies of size and scale also arise when translating designs into cross stitch where, of necessity, everything must be over-simplified. The general rule to follow is, if you like it and want to put it on your own sampler, go ahead.

OTHER PICTORIAL MOTIFS

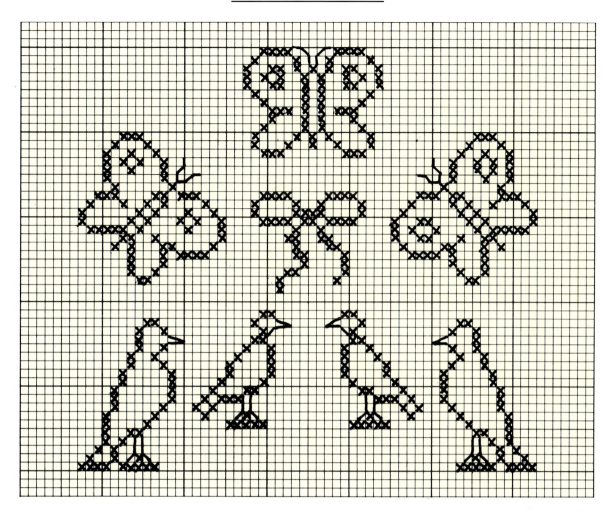

53 Birds and butterflies

Centring a motif

When you add spot motifs or initials to the sampler you can place them randomly, or you can plan at graph paper stage to put them accurately at the centre of the space available. The formula for centring a motif is as follows:

1. Count the number of squares across in the area where the motif will fit (a).
2. Count the number of squares (i.e. stitches) occupied by the motif (b).
3. Deduct (b) from (a).
4. Divide the result by two. The resulting figure shows the number of squares to leave blank on either side of the motif.
5. Repeat steps (1)–(4) for the vertical spaces available.
6. At sewing stage, count the pairs of threads accordingly.

Doing this simple arithmetic will enable you to place motifs or initials exactly where they will look most effective.

Other stitches

You could also vary your stitches at this stage by introducing petit point, french knots, or four-sided stitch.

Petit point is a diagonal stitch made over a single thread; you could use a cross stitch or just half a cross stitch. You will achieve a very fine effect and will immediately drastically reduce your rate of progress, as more and more options are open to you with this stitch. I tend to use it only in very small areas, for example for the hanging basket in the garden gift sampler shown in chapter 6. Perhaps I was put off using petit point because the first embroidery kit I purchased was a small design in petit point which took ages to complete and was, I now realize, far too complex for a beginner to attempt. You need very good eyesight and a lot of patience to do much petit point work, but it is certainly worth an experiment or two.

If you look on old samplers featuring figures and worked over double threads of canvas, you can sometimes find that when the embroiderers came to the face, and needed more detail, they split the double canvas and worked the features in petit point over single threads. This procedure was known as 'pricking the ground'.

Another variation which gives a lighter, lacy effect is to replace one cross stitch with four back stitches in a square taking up the same space. This can give additional texture in a single-colour area, or added contrast if worked in a different colour. It could be used if you had worked cross stitch in a very pale colour but found the stitch did not stand out from the background. A dark outline, possibly worked with a single thread in four sided stitch, could be just the thing to make that pale highlight stand out.

French knots will give a lacy textured appearance and can be used for flowers or foliage. The trees on my *No place like home* sampler in the colour photographs are french knots, and the stitches stand up quite satisfyingly. I have tried for years to make a stitch diagram for a french knot, but it is still one thing that I think really needs to be demonstrated in person. However, an attempt at a stitch diagram is shown here if you cannot find an expert to show you how to work it.

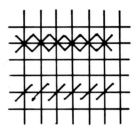

54 Petit point. Cross stitches and half cross stitches formed over a single fabric thread

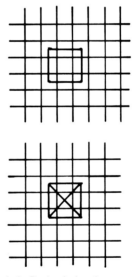

55 Four-sided stitch. Back stitches in a square worked over two threads each; and a single cross stitch outlined with four-sided stitch

WORKING WITH SEVERAL COLOURS

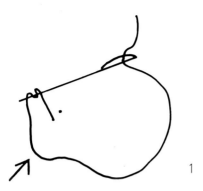

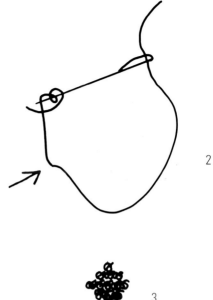

56 Forming a french knot.
  1. Bring thread up from reverse. Hold needle above fabric, hold thread where shown by arrow. Wind thread twice round point of needle
  2. Keep holding thread at arrow. Re-insert needle two threads away. Feed needle through loops – french knot will form on surface
  3. Finished group of french knots gives a good texture

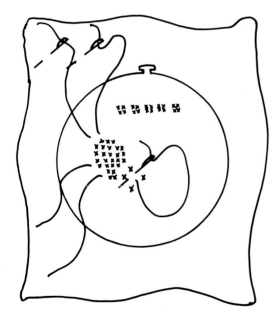

57 Working with several colours. Bring other colours up to surface when not in use. Use more than one needle if you like

Working with several colours

When you sew the pictorial part of your sampler, you may be using a larger number of colours. I added three more colours – gold and two shades of green – to mine. I also achieved a mottled effect on the two cats by mixing colours on the needle; I used one strand each of red and gold for the left-hand cat, and one strand each of dark brown and blue for the right-hand cat.

If you are sewing a motif containing several colours, you can avoid tangles on the back, or tedious stopping and starting, by bringing the coloured threads not in use up to the front of the work where you can see them. Take them out to one side and then pick up and re-thread the needle with each colour as you require it. You could of course use several needles, one for each colour, to save rethreading.

WORKING WITH SEVERAL COLOURS

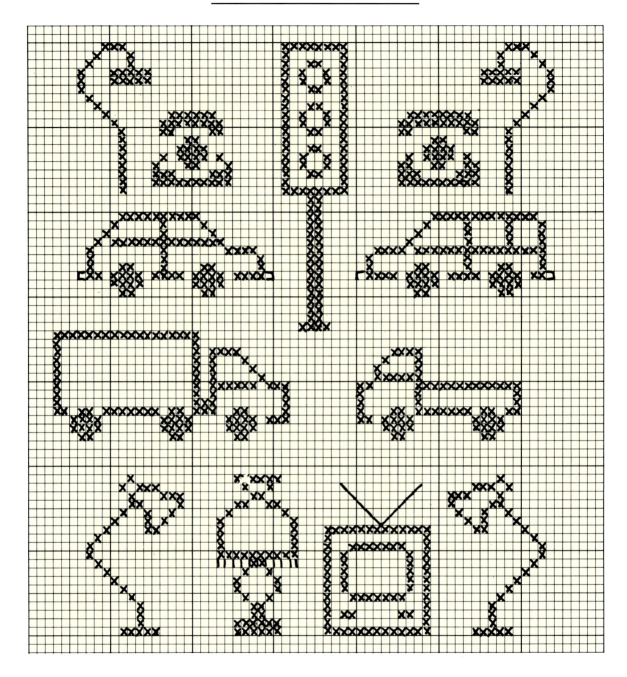

58 Some modern doodles

As you reach the finishing stages of this central part of your first sampler I hope your mind will be full of new ideas. If you still have some small spaces to fill you can be much more free and less disciplined with the pictorial section and even depart from the chart if you wish – why not? There is no need to stick to traditional motifs, either; we are living in the twentieth century, so why not include something up-to-date? As traditional samplers may have reflected the life of their day, it is only reasonable for us to include some motifs

WORKING WITH SEVERAL COLOURS

to represent our own lives. The doodles here represent more modern subjects such as transport, electricity and communications, to get you started.

You may well feel disappointed that not all your ideas can be accommodated, but please remember that this simple sampler has been designed as a first project and is therefore very small. It is hoped that it will not be the only sampler you will make. Now you have grasped the basics of marking out the fabric and counting stitches and spaces you are quite capable of planning out another, and possibly more ambitious, sampler. I know I have never yet been truly and completely satisfied with any sampler I have sewn; there is always room somewhere for improvement or something I would do differently another time.

Lastly, don't forget to include your name or initials and the date; it is always possible you may have created an heirloom for generations yet to come.

CHAPTER 4

Borders

As you finish the pictorial part of your sampler you will see that it is crying out for some sort of border. The border is as important, if not more important, than the central part of the sampler and there are several choices open to you.

Before you start, one piece of good news. You do not need to chart tediously around the complete sampler when planning the border; this is where the tacking threads marking the centres and the rectangle come into their own. If you chart one quarter of the border, taking the original threads which marked half-way down and across as your guide, the other three quarters of the border will be mirror images. However, a continuous border needs to fit accurately; if you start sewing blithely at a fancy border and trust to luck that it will fit properly, the chances are that it will not!

We need only to look at historical samplers to see that they, also, were started from the centre with the border fitted on last. Quite often all four corners are different, and it is interesting to see how adjustments have been made in fitting the borders round. Problems can arise at the corners where the sides and top meet, or don't quite meet, which is when adjustments are called for. If the corners are not right, this will be glaringly obvious, to you, if not to everyone else. However, there are several solutions and with a little forward planning you can find and use a border which will enhance your work.

If you make further samplers you can consider planning the border at an earlier stage to make sure that problems with corners can be avoided before they arise, but for a first sampler the border would have been an illogical and confusing place to start.

Decisions need to be made on various points before choosing a border. I know you feel you have nearly finished your sampler and can't wait to see it mounted, framed and up on the wall, but please take a little time to choose the right border. A bit of work with pencil and graph paper at this stage can save a lot of unpicking and frustration later on, or a mistake left on for all to see (fig 61).

On the *Home Sweet Home* sampler (you can see it with its border finished on page 80) I have made a simple crenellated border with a decorative corner and outlined it with two rows of cross stitches to improve its appearance. A border can be plain or fancy and some samplers consist almost entirely of borders. The *Noel* Christmas card design (in the final chapter) was worked as an exercise in placing borders, but with a first sampler simplicity is probably a good idea.

BORDERS

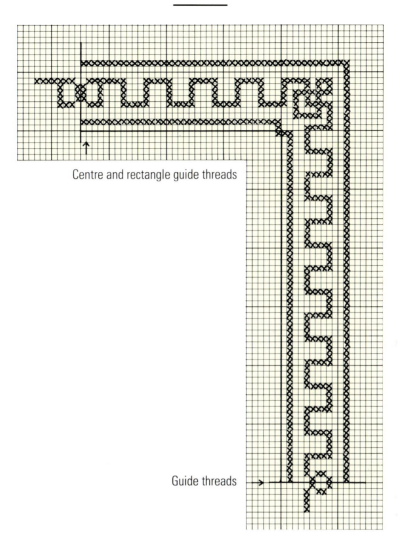

Centre and rectangle guide threads

Guide threads

A counted continuous border

If you wish to use a continuous border all around the work you will need to ensure that that the stitches fit exactly into your guide threads at the central part of a motif.

I have counted and charted some suitable borders to fit your rectangle size in figs 62–64 and you can see that, as for the decorative motifs in the body of the sampler, if the border motifs are made up of an even number of stitches, the cross stitches can butt up to the guide threads to make the border fit exactly around the work. An example of this is the simple border of boxes in fig 62.

59 Chart for one quarter of border. Mark guidelines to represent one quarter of rectangle (35 × 60 squares). Start charting border at corner. Mark along sides. If border does not fit precisely where it crosses centre guide threads, make a small adjustment as shown

However, it is often the case that the motifs contain an odd number of stitches. As before, you need to make the fine adjustment of straddling the centre stitch over the guideline to achieve a symmetrical balance (*see* figs 63 and 64). This adjustment needs to be made for both sides and top, so you can see that careful thought is needed before you place the first stitch.

BORDERS

60 One quarter of border stitched

BORDERS

61 Sampler featuring imaginary date and age as an excuse for the badly counted border

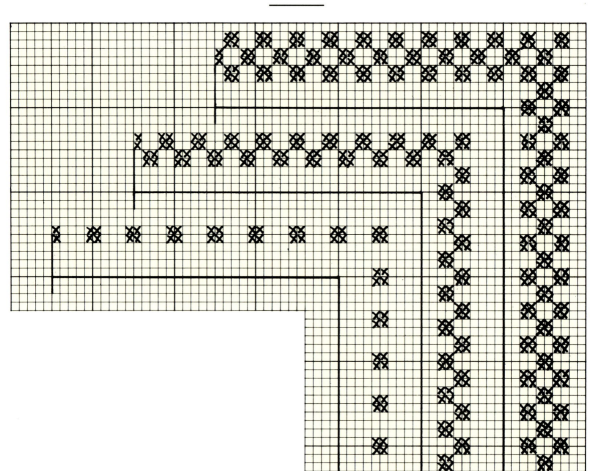

62 Continuous borders based on boxes. Charted to fit outline 35 × 60 stitches. Ruled line represents rectangle tacking line. Butt cross stitches up to centre line

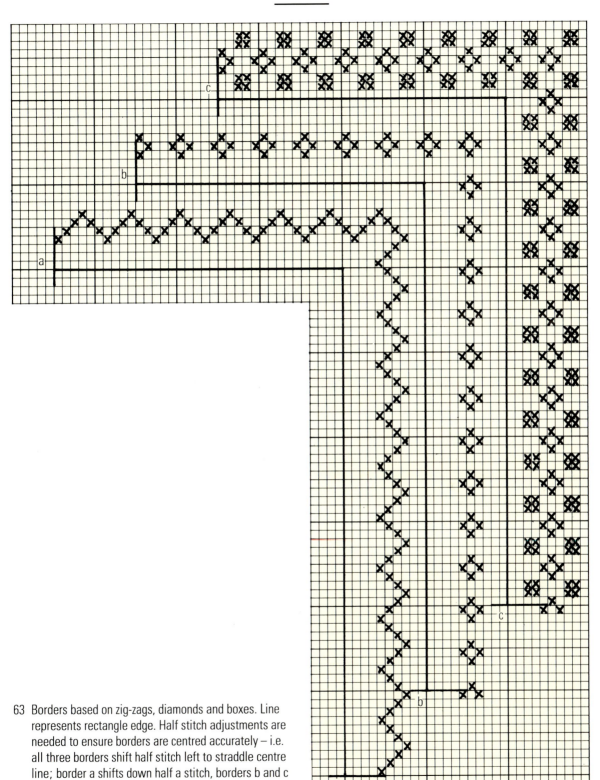

63 Borders based on zig-zags, diamonds and boxes. Line represents rectangle edge. Half stitch adjustments are needed to ensure borders are centred accurately – i.e. all three borders shift half stitch left to straddle centre line; border a shifts down half a stitch, borders b and c shift up half a stitch

BORDERS

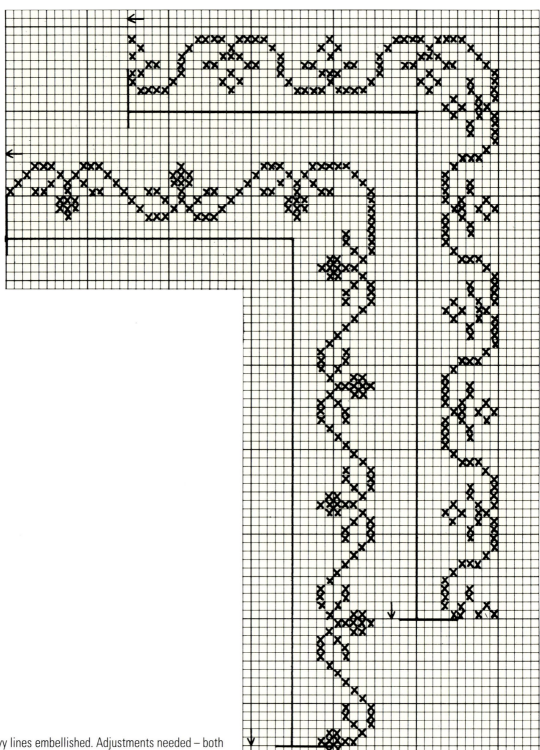

64 Wavy lines embellished. Adjustments needed – both borders half stitch left, half stitch down

BORDERS

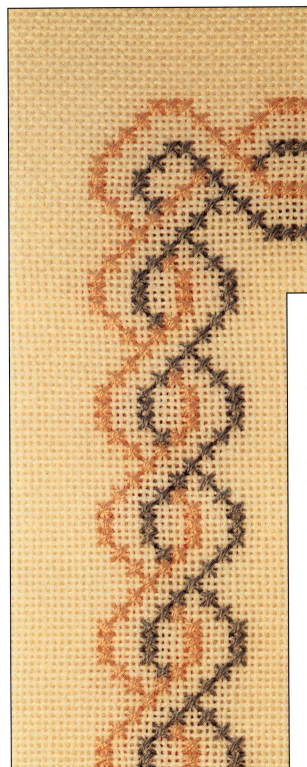

A corner from a continuous border

You can see from fig 64 that some borders have a simple foundation line which can then be embellished and can take on several forms. If you then add the extra dimension of colour to these, you have the basis of a very pleasing border. You can base your border choice on one of the charted borders and then dress it up to your heart's content.

If you wish to plot out your own original continuous border to fit the outline we are using (one quarter is 35 stitches across and 60 down) here is how to go about it:

First, draw guidelines on the graph paper 35 squares by 60 squares to represent the edge of sampler worked so far. Then work out how far away from the body of the sampler you wish to place the border.

Count diagonally from the corner and start plotting out Xs at the corner with a shape that pleases you. Continue down the side and across the top and see where your design motif meets the guidelines, marking centres. Does it fit nicely? If yes, you can go ahead and sew. If not, you need to make some adjustments.

BORDERS

If the difference is very small, perhaps you can shift the whole border up or down or across a little. If the final border ends up five stitches away from the sides of the rectangle but only three stitches away from the top or bottom, it will still appear acceptable, and this is one way you can 'juggle' to make the border fit.

However, if the corner is lovely, but the border motif just will not fit tidily on to the centre threads, a good way around the problem is used in the example shown. Start plotting the border from the top corner and work along to the centres of the sides and top. When you get near to the problem at the centre guide threads, where it does not fit perfectly, just put in a different motif, one which will fit. You can see from fig 59 that my crenellated squarish border breaks into a different shape at centre top and centre sides; I hope it looks as though that was intended all along! This is just one example of how adjustments can be made to avoid problems at the corners.

Easier border solutions

If working out corners and adjustments seems too fiddly for you at this stage, there are other solutions.

Straight lines all round: an extremely simple border which involves no counting at all. Arrange several lines of cross stitch round the sampler as a border, each line being a different colour, preferably the colours used in the body of the sampler. Experiment with coloured pencils until you decide which combination and arrangement of colours is most effective. You can space the lines equal distances apart, or vary the spacing if you wish. Although there is not much counting involved, there is quite a bit of stitching, especially if you use several colours. This border may take longer than you think to sew.

Rectangles and corners: you could treat the border as four separate rectangles placed around the body of your sampler. You could outline these in cross or back stitch, or merely mark them on the fabric with tacking threads and use one of the bands of decorative motifs to fill in the space. Then you need something different to finish off the corners and I have suggested some simple geometric ideas. If you get out the graph paper and start doodling I am sure you can find something simple and effective for corner motifs. If you use this method you may like to enclose your rectangles and corner motifs inside a solid line of cross stitches or back stitches; this will give the border more unity and impact and also does not need counting. Use the guide threads already on the fabric to start sewing the decorative motifs at the centre, then they will balance nicely and look symmetrical.

Suggested border, using rectangles and separate corner motifs. No need to count: use guide threads to place outlines accurately

65 Treating sides as separate rectangles

BORDERS

66 Rectangles with corner motifs

BORDERS

Back stitch border: using a back stitch border also avoids too much thread counting. The one illustrated here features interest at centres and corners but was not difficult to sew. I charted the top centre and one corner motif first. When I came to sew I started at the centre, using the guide threads to place the first stitches. Next I worked the corner motif, again locating the correct place by referring to chart and guide threads. Then I joined the two together with the single back stitch line and continued down the sides. Although the border looks quite complicated it did not involve too much planning and was simple and very quick to sew.

U-shaped border: it could be that you have seen a really fancy old border which you would like to copy, but you just cannot seem to make it fit round. Often the two top corners seem to work but the third, and especially the fourth corner present a problem. Well, you could study and chart this border to fit across the top of your work and down the sides to somewhere near the bottom. Then, what about stopping it there and avoiding the problem of the third and fourth corners by putting something different along the bottom edge of the sampler? Perhaps this could be the name of your town, or a row of floral motifs. Use whatever seems to fit in with the rest of the work. This inverted U-border is really just another variation of the rectangles and corner motifs.

As you can see, there is plenty to think about when planning the border, the finishing touch to your work. The question of colour will also arise. Throughout I have tried to keep to just a few colours to make stitching simple and to speed your progress. You will need to choose colours for the border; perhaps you will choose the dominant colour from the rest of the sampler, or a two or three colour combination, which will open up even more possibilities. At this stage you may feel that the whole work needs jazzing up a little and calls for a colourful border treatment. Alternatively, you may decide that a really quiet border is needed to tone down a colourful central treatment. It's up to you!

Presentation

Another thing to consider at the border stage is the eventual presentation of the work. Sampler sewing on evenweave fabric has an enormous advantage over canvas work in that the embroidery does not need to be measured exactly to fit inside a frame. The fabric itself, unstitched, is very attractive, so the simplest possible treatment is available as an option; just mount and lace the sampler over board and slip it into a picture frame.

If you decide to have your sampler framed professionally, it is a good idea to have a treatment in mind before you visit the picture framer, as his ideas may not coincide with yours. A picture framer should be a skilled person who will recommend a suitable deep frame and who will be able to cut a tidy mitre for the corners (no easy task, as do-it-yourselfers will probably already know), and also make a neat chamfered cut on mounting board if you should decide to display your sampler under a coloured mount.

If you are more economy-minded, you don't need to have a frame specially made. You can buy a ready-made frame, or even a picture – my students haunt the cheap picture stalls on the local market, looking not at the pictures, but at the frames! When you do your research you will see that it is often cheaper to buy a

East West – Home's Best. Illustrates back stitch border treatment, although the mixed colour alphabet and the motto layout are not so successful

FINISHING, MOUNTING AND FRAMING

finished picture and take it apart for the frame, than it is to buy picture-framing wood and make the frame yourself. Car boot sales are also rich hunting grounds for old picture and photograph frames and, of course, these can give an 'antique' effect, if that is what you are seeking.

Finishing, mounting and framing

Once the border is complete, there are just a few things more you need to do to finish off your sampler. Don't forget to remove the tacked guide threads; they have been useful to you but you don't need them any more. Tidy up the loose ends on the back of the work; long straggling ends on the back will, unfortunately, show through the fabric, especially if they are of a dark colour.

Your work may have become soiled during working and need washing. I try to avoid washing samplers but the fabric and threads should be colour-fast and washable, with gentle treatment. Use a mild detergent and

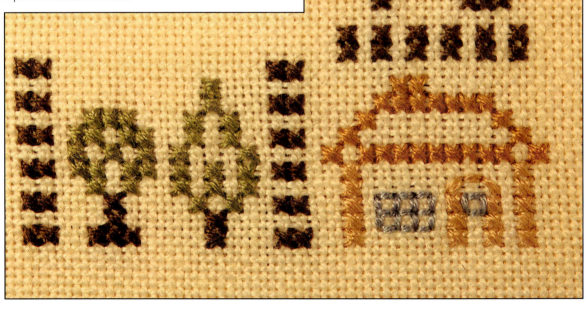

A pictorial border of houses

FINISHING, MOUNTING AND FRAMING

lukewarm water and do not squeeze or wring; just think how this could distort your carefully sewn cross stitches. Just swoosh it gently around in the washing solution, rinse well, and dry flat on a towel, away from direct heat.

Many books tell you not to press finished cross stitch work as it flattens the stitches. However, I find that by this stage the fabric itself is quite crumpled, so I normally compromise by pressing lightly under a damp clean cloth, concentrating more on the unworked fabric and skimming lightly over the stitched areas.

You will need to know your frame size before you cut a piece of board on which to mount your work, so that the sampler will fit nicely inside the frame. It is recommended that samplers are mounted over hardboard, but as the dark colour would spoil the appearance of the work, making it look dingy, you will first need to cover the hardboard with light coloured fabric – white sheeting or something similar would be ideal, and it is best to stick to natural fibres.

I must confess that I usually use a piece of white mounting board and lace my samplers over that. If I cannot find white I use a coloured board and stick white paper on to it for a light effect. However, using cardboard may well be storing up problems for the future: cardboard can attract damp which might cause damage or discolouration, and may contain acids which could damage the work as the years pass. So, if you want your sampler to survive into the twenty-first century or beyond, it is worthwhile spending a little time getting it right, using the hardboard and a piece of white fabric as the foundation on which to lace your work.

67 Remove tacked guide threads

68 Tidy up loose ends

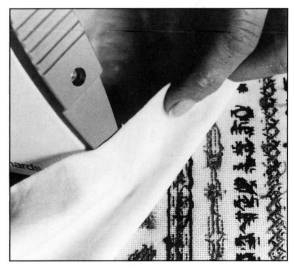

69 Lightly press face down under a damp cloth

FINISHING, MOUNTING AND FRAMING

I work at the ironing board when mounting the sampler over the board. Starting with the sampler face down, lay the board centrally over the fabric and then turn the sampler face up, with the board underneath. This sounds complicated, but I find that by starting this way it is easier to place the board accurately in position. Use a ruler to measure that the top, bottom and side margins are symmetrical, and follow the fabric threads to make absolutely sure that the sampler is sitting straight over the board. You need to be very accurate as a crookedly mounted sampler will be very irritating to you (I do know, from experience). Place pins at the board edges through the fabric so that they stick out and you can turn over the work with pins still in place (*see* fig 72). Check carefully once again that sampler is centrally over the board and then turn the work over again so that the sampler is face down.

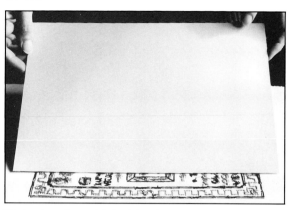

70 Lay board over fabric, fabric face down

71 Turn right side up and measure to see that board is placed accurately and symmetrically

72 Pin edges as shown, then turn work face down

FINISHING, MOUNTING AND FRAMING

I like to mitre the corners of fabric when turning it in over the board as I find this reduces bulk and makes for a neater finish, without having to take the drastic step of cutting fabric away. Fold in the corner and then the sides to make a neat mitre and pin with pins facing inwards towards the centre. Repeat this procedure with all four corners; one reason I use the ironing board is that I can walk around it to do the pinning, which avoids disturbing the sampler during the process.

When all four corners are pinned, thread up your needle with strong thread, anchor firmly (this is the only time I allow myself to start off with a knot, or loop) at one corner and, using large stitches, catch the edges of the mitre together. Sew along the mitre, then lace across to pull in the sides as shown, finishing this length of thread at the diagonal opposite corner. Repeat for the other two corners. Your sampler should be firmly and neatly mounted over the card, ready for the frame.

If using glass please don't forget to clean it thoroughly on both sides, because when the sampler is on the wall it will be too late to remove that little speck you find so annoying.

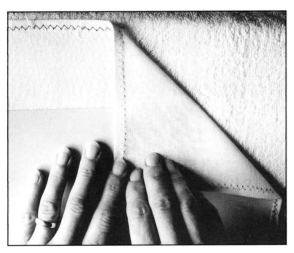

73 Fold in first corner

74 Fold in first side for mitre

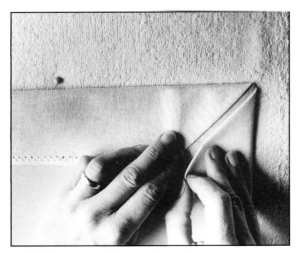

75 Fold in second side to complete mitre

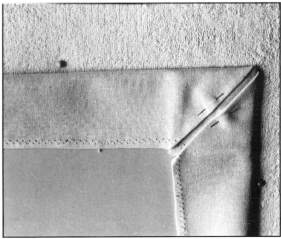

76 First corner, mitred and pinned

FINISHING, MOUNTING AND FRAMING

If you use a shallow picture frame you may find that the bulk of glass, fabric, hardboard, sheeting and backing paper will not sit neatly in the frame. I find a few tacks and a lot of very strong tape will hold everything quite firmly in place.

Then your work is finished and you can hang your framed sampler up on the wall and wait for the admiring comments. Choose a large wall and hopefully it will soon be joined by other samplers in your own private display.

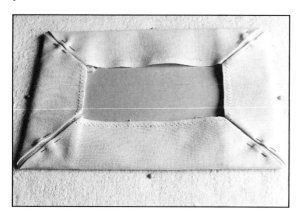

77 Corners pinned with pins facing inwards towards centre

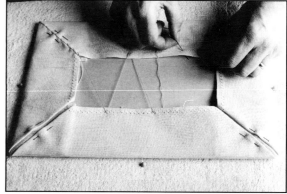

78 Using strong thread, start sewing edges together at corner

79 Pull thread firmly to hold fabric taut

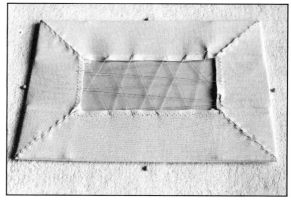

80 Complete lacing across, then remove pins

FINISHING, MOUNTING AND FRAMING

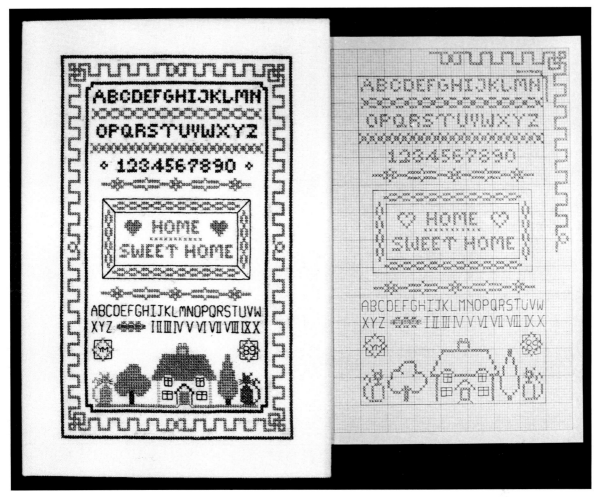

81 The simple sampler finished and mounted, compared with original chart

The simple sampler worked stage by stage in Chapters 1–4

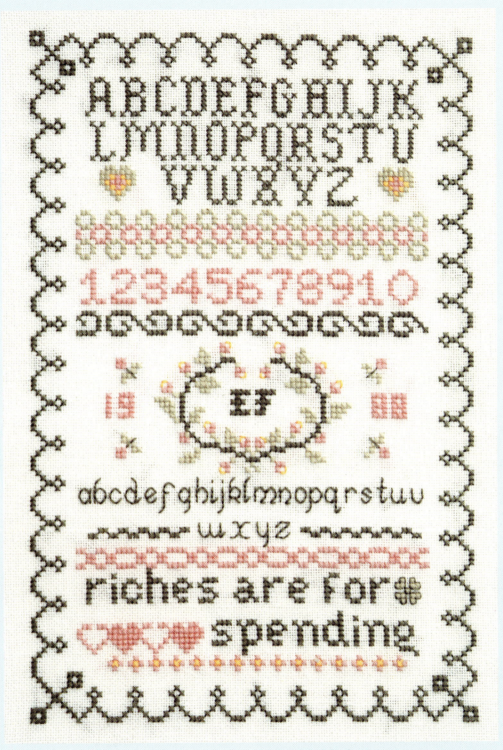

Riches are for Spending by Eve Fuller. Standard rectangle, with yellow used sparingly for highlights

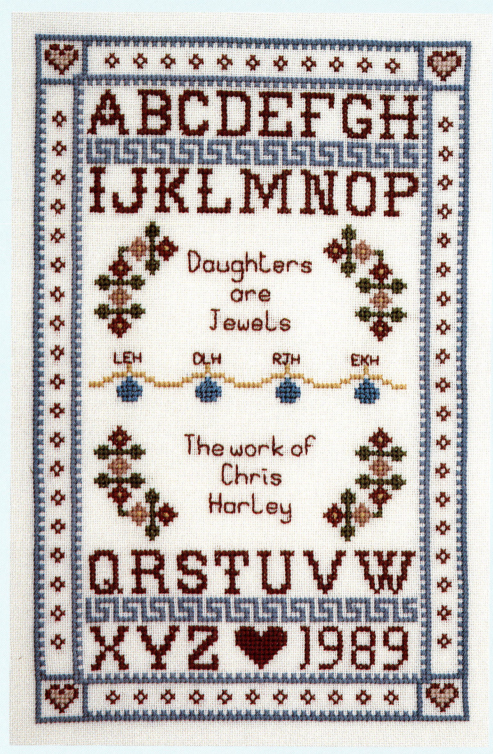

Daughters are Jewels by Chris Harley. Standard rectangle, with a metallic thread used for the 'jewels'.

Labours Accomplished are Pleasant by Dorothy Banham. Family names feature in the trees around the farmhouse

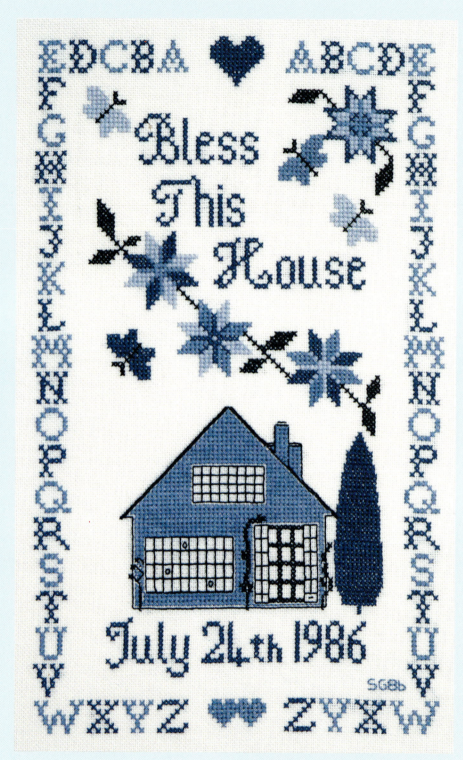

Bless this House by Sally Gilding. The alphabet, worked in two directions, is used as the border

Boston sampler. Large alphabet based on a French sampler. Other stitches, eg. herringbone, are featured; back stitch is used in the decorative bands

Decorative alphabet from a design source book by Anne Rainey. Oversize house bricks make for a primitive effect

No Place like Home. Worked in back stitch using single thread for very small scale details. The trees are worked with French knots

A large sampler (24 × 39cm/10 × 15 in) by Sally Gilding. A selection of ten alphabets, with clever pictorial motifs

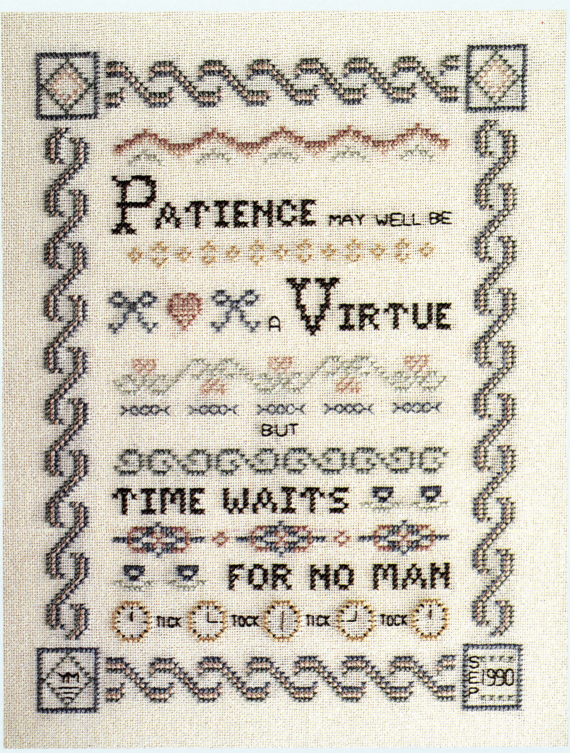

Patience sampler. The border is based on ancient Roman mosaic border (guilloche) shapes

Work in progress. 'P is for photography' is part of a proposed alphabet quilt including embroidered panels, by Andy Mathieson. He has included himself, his camera equipment and a picture of the house on this small panel. He works quite freely, which lends spontaneity to the piece

CHAPTER 5

Blackwork basics

Some experiments in blackwork embroidery are a logical progression from making a first sampler. You can use the same fabric, threads and needles to get started.

Blackwork embroidery is thought to have originated in the East, which could account for the repeating Moorish and Arabic designs which feature in some of the motifs, and seems to have come to England via Spain around the time that Katherine of Aragon arrived to marry the Prince of Wales.

The double running stitch used is also sometimes called Holbein stitch for the (perhaps rather dubious) reason that Holbein painted a famous portrait of Henry VIII looking very portly and wearing rich garments elegantly decorated with blackwork embroidery. Some of Holbein's other portraits also feature blackwork on the garments of his sitters.

Blackwork embroidery uses only one colour (usually, but not necessarily, black) and relies for its decorative effect on shapes and shadings, which are achieved by sewing tiny repeating motifs. A symmetrical effect is achieved by counting the threads on evenweave fabric, in the same manner as for cross stitch samplers, but, as you can see, the stitches can go in any direction and be of varying lengths, so many more possibilities are opened up for us.

As an illustration, consider the space taken up by a single cross stitch, worked over two threads. Look closely and you will see that there are, in the same space, *nine* holes in the fabric. So curved effects and scrolls no longer present the problems they did when designing for cross stitch on this very small scale.

Sewing a blackwork sampler

If you regard blackwork embroidery as a separate art medium, as with any new style of embroidery, a stitch sampler is a very good place to start. You may find you wish to make this into a finished article to hang on the wall (see Dorothy Banham's sampler – fig 82), or you may prefer to use the sampler to try out new ideas and then incorporate them into a different work, perhaps a blackwork picture.

Unlike the formal cross stitch sampler, you don't need to chart out this random sampler, although the graph paper and pencil will be very useful for doodles and trying out ideas. It's a good idea to take a piece of evenweave fabric (same size 50 cm × 40 cm (20 in × 15 in)), hem the edges, mark the centre point by two lines of tacking stitches (we may wish to add on a border later) and start anywhere at random.

You will soon find out that compact shapes

SEWING A BLACKWORK SAMPLER

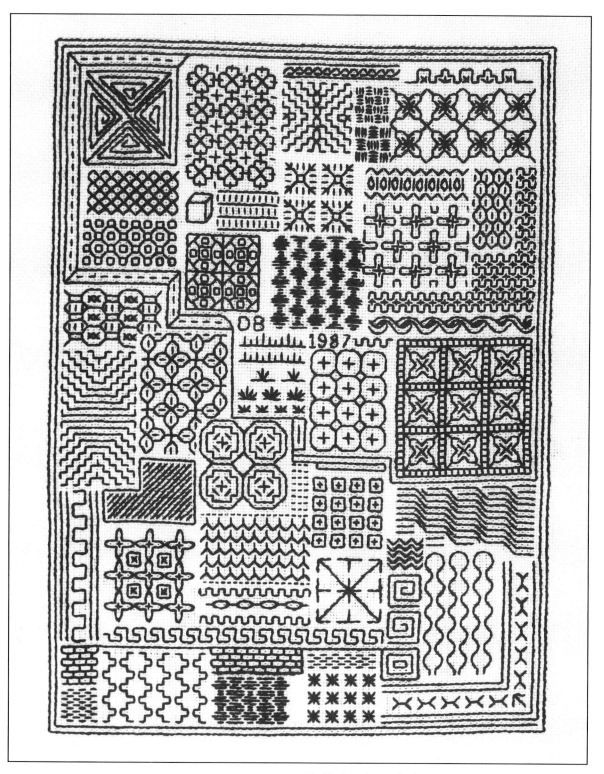

82 Blackwork sampler by Dorothy Banham

SEWING A BLACKWORK SAMPLER

and small stitches give a dense shading effect (fig 83), whereas open shapes with longer lines give a lighter tone (fig 84). Photographers who work in black and white generally agree that there are ten tones of grey they can reproduce, but workers in blackwork embroidery have an almost unlimited range of tones at their disposal.

Threads

As well as varying the shapes and sizes of motifs you also have a new range of threads to work with. As you know, the stranded cotton itself can be used in six different thread weights (using one strand on the needle, up to six strands). There are also threads manufactured specifically for blackwork. The *coton à broder* 16 is a fine thread and pleasant to use, and black cotton perle threads graduate through grades 8, 5 and 3 (a heavy thread difficult to pass through the fabric threads). Committed blackwork embroiderers spend their time haunting embroidery shops looking for yet another thread weight for yet another effect.

83 Some compact shapes making dense tones

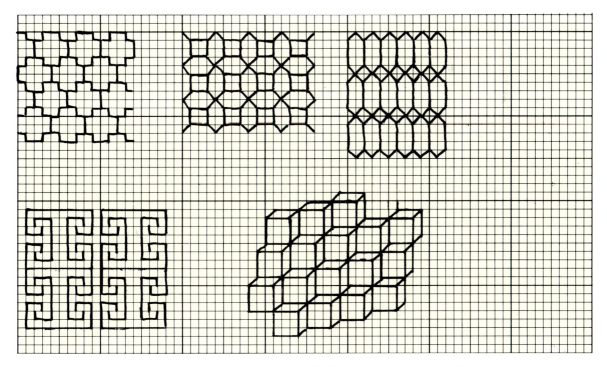

84 Some larger shapes for medium tones

Stitches

Traditionally, a double running stitch was used for blackwork – out with a running stitch, turn around, and return filling in the gaps – but I sometimes find I get a bit 'lost' when working a complicated motif with this stitch. I prefer to use back stitch and complete one stitch at a time; at least you can keep a check on how the motif is progressing. I normally work over two threads, either diagonally or across, but of course you can vary this with shorter or longer stitches if these suit the shape you choose.

85 Threads for blackwork

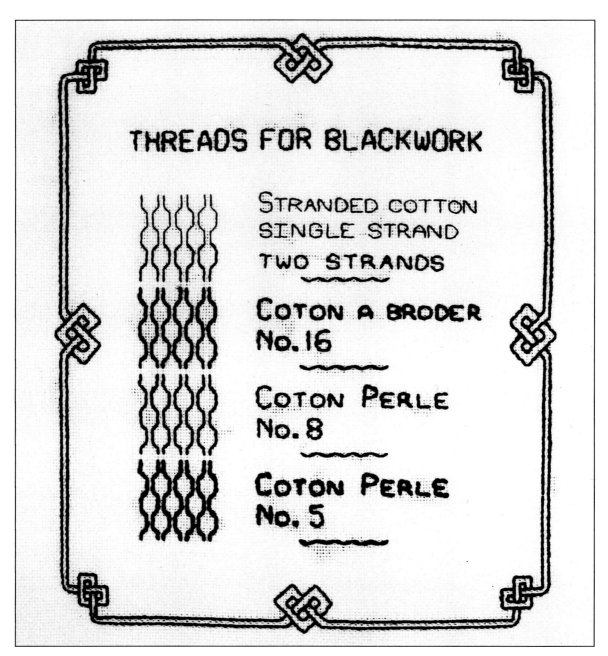

USING BLACKWORK MOTIFS

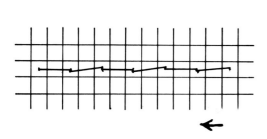 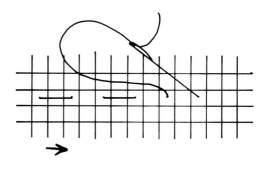

Motifs

On with the sampler. The fabric is prepared, the needle is threaded; which motif will you choose? Once again the pencil and graph paper are useful here or you could work a motif from the suggestions that follow. Try working with one strand of thread on the needle and then, each time you re-thread, try something different. Keep the threads in use quite short so they will not wear or go fuzzy.

This is the time to look around for ideas and start collecting for the scrapbook. You will find that once you 'get your eye in' ideas abound all around. Floor and wall tiles are often rich design sources for repeating patterns, sometimes put together in very clever ways. I have shown some graph paper doodles based on the same single unit in three different arrangements (fig 87).

Fig 102 shows another motif based on floor tiles, first shown straight on and then turned on to its side. The photographs in this chapter contain several motif ideas to get you started.

Using blackwork motifs

Simple motifs alone can be very effective – indeed some blackwork pictures rely on only one or two shapes – but if you look at fig 89 you can see how a motif can be developed from a very simple start into something altogether more complex. The fun comes in finding out where to stop!

Having chosen a few motifs and tried them

86 Double running stitch.
   1st row work right to left, each stitch over two fabric threads. Turn and return, filling in gaps.
   Note: each stitch on the return journey comes up on one side of first row stitch (in same hole) and goes in on the other side. Effect exaggerated on diagram, but actually results in a straight line

out on the fabric, where hopefully the wobbly drawn lines will now be straight, another experiment is to change the way in which the motifs are linked together, or to make small adjustments to the pattern. This can cause a big difference in the overall effect, sometimes in quite unexpected ways.

Geometric shapes

One of my own favourite shapes is the octagon and I have used this for my experiments, joining octagons together in different ways. The shapes can be further filled in with cross stitches if desired.

The octagon shape also illustrates one important fact if you sew a shape which includes both straight and diagonal lines, it will soon become apparent that a stitch over two threads formed diagonally is longer than a stitch formed over two threads horizontally or vertically.

This variation is unimportant when sewing on a very small scale but needs to be taken into consideration if you are forming geometric shapes on a larger scale, as I did in the firescreen shown here (fig 91). If you want all the sides of the octagon to be equal, you need

USING BLACKWORK MOTIFS

87 Design from floor tile: single tile linked together in three different ways

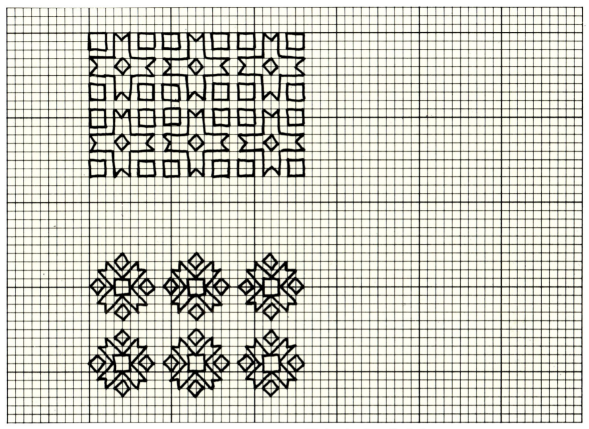

88 Another floor tile design

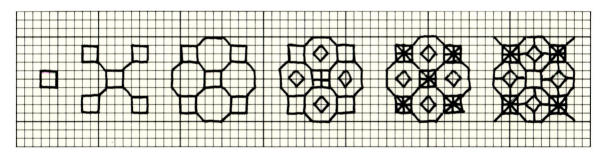

to count fewer stitches diagonally than vertically or horizontally. The enlarged octagon shown in fig 92 illustrates this, and expresses the proportion you need to bear in mind; there should be two-thirds the number of diagonal stitches to horizontal or vertical stitches, in order to keep the shape in proportion and looking 'right'. It took me some time to discover this, and if I had listened harder to geometry lessons in school I

89 Blackwork motif developed from simple to complex shape

could probably explain the reason for this in mathematical terms. Suffice it to say that geometric shapes filled with blackwork motifs can be a very good basis for embroidered pieces. There are a variety to choose from, starting from a simple square.

USING BLACKWORK MOTIFS

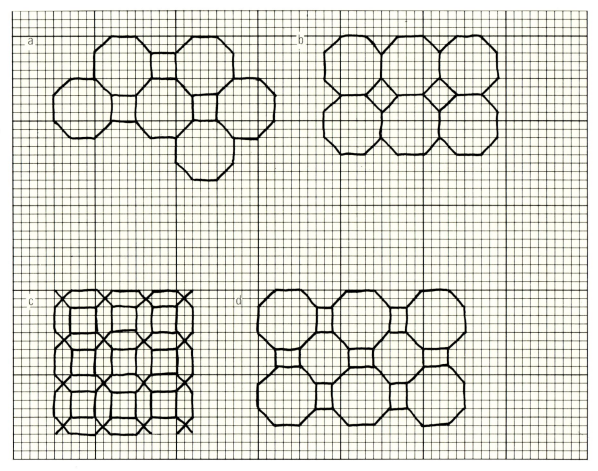

90 Octagons linked together in different ways.
(a) Joined by their diagonal sides – squares form in the middle;
(b) joined by their straight sides – diamonds form in the middle;
(c) overlapping – how many other patterns form?
(d) placed apart and linked by straight lines – smaller octagons form in the middle

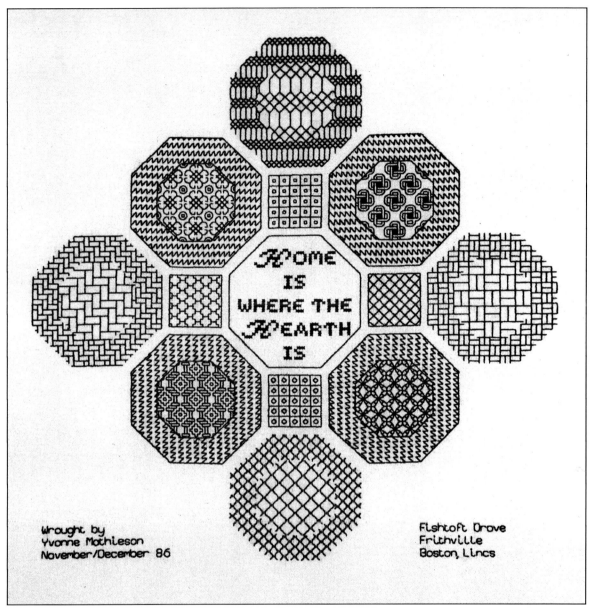

91 Blackwork firescreen

USING BLACKWORK MOTIFS

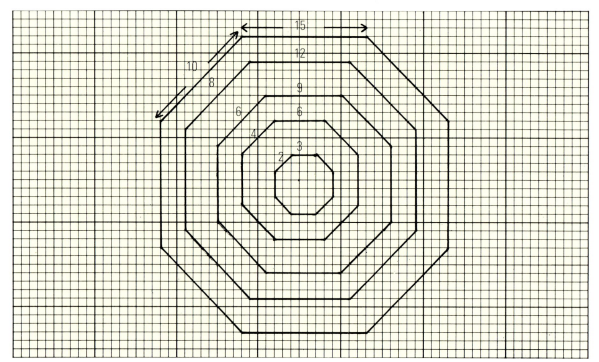

Many blackwork samplers of the past have been in the form of a chequerboard – Sally Gilding has worked an excellent example of this – or you could use triangles, rectangles, octagons, etc. At this stage, beware of the hexagon, as you could struggle trying to fit a hexagon (which has a basis of 60 degree angles) on to this essentially right-angled fabric. Having gained some experience by sewing the blackwork sampler you may wish to produce a blackwork embroidery in this geometric style. Beware of starting on a very large project; it is frustrating to start something and then tire of it before it is finished.

92 Enlarged octagons. To stay in proportion, diagonal stitches need to cover two-thirds the number of threads to the number covered by horizontals and verticals

USING BLACKWORK MOTIFS

93 Chequerboard sampler by Sally Gilding

Making blackwork pictures

Planning a design

You may wish to depart from the geometric discipline and make a blackwork picture by basing your project on a photograph, postcard or greetings card.

If you cut a black and white photograph out of the newspaper and study it under a magnifying glass you will see that it is made up of thousands of tiny dots. These are dense where the image is dark and more sparse in the paler areas. A useful exercise is to take this photograph and imagine that you are going to make a blackwork interpretation using, for simplicity's sake, just five different shades of grey, e.g. light, medium-light, medium, medium-dark and dark. You will also have white at your disposal; the area of fabric you leave unworked.

Now, take a pencil and draw an outline around different areas of shading on your photograph. Can you decide which areas should be darkest? Draw a line around them. Carry on for each shade until you have

94 Blackwork rosebud worked on Aida fabric: design based on a greetings card

USING BLACKWORK PICTURES

decided on a treatment for each area of the photograph.

You can also plan blackwork embroidery by using cut-up pieces of newsprint sorted into different densities. This method has the advantage that you can move them around until you are satisfied with the effect achieved. Personally, I can never find newsprint with the right print density and I seem to get printers' ink all over my hands. Also, I seem to have trouble relating these scraps of paper to a finished embroidery (I am more likely to start reading the news stories) so I tend not to use this method, although it has been well tried and tested by others. At the planning stage it is enough to be able to 'see' in shades of grey and to experiment on the sampler with various effects.

The procedure for translating a picture into shapes works equally well for blackwork embroidery, cross stitch or canvas work.

Translating a picture into a workable project

Find a picture that appeals to you in a newspaper, magazine, greetings card, postcard, etc. Alternatively, you could draw an original if you prefer. Choose one which has strong shapes so it will 'translate' well into embroidery. Trace the outline shapes from the original on to tracing or greaseproof paper. Then you have a choice of methods as follows.

Method 1 – the chart

Transfer the traced outlines on to graph paper as described on page 48. Make a chart, suggesting treatments and blackwork motifs for the outlined areas. If you have worked out motifs on a sampler, there is no need to chart them out again tediously; just make a note of which motif you intend to use in each area. Following the chart and counting threads, use tacking cotton to mark round the outlines on the fabric.

Method 2 – from tracing direct to fabric

You will need a special water-erasable pen for this method, available from craft shops. Do test it first on a spare piece of fabric to convince yourself that it washes away without leaving a trace. This could avoid tears later. Place the tracing face up on a light coloured table or on a piece of white card. Lay the evenweave fabric over the top and you should be able to see the design lines showing through. Pin the fabric to the tracing paper, follow the design lines carefully with the water-erasable pen, and there is your outline design transferred to the fabric.

You could also use daylight and a window for this exercise. Tape the tracing to the inside surface of a light window and tape the fabric over it. The design can then be seen quite clearly against the daylight and drawn round with the water-erasable pen.

Method 3 – dressmakers' carbon paper

Lay the fabric on the table, carbon paper next, inky side down, and tracing on top. Go over the outlines in pencil once more and the carbon paper will transfer a line on to your fabric. This will wash away when the work is finished provided you do use dressmakers' carbon which is designed for this.

Method 4 – tracing paper and tacking threads

Trace the design and pin the tracing paper over the fabric. Now tack through both paper and fabric, following the outlines. If you place your tacking stitches a fraction to one side of the pencil line, you will avoid transferring unwelcome pencil marks on to your fabric. When you finish tacking, carefully tear away the paper, leaving the tacked outlines on the fabric.

Selecting blackwork motifs

If you have not already done so, you will need

MAKING BLACKWORK PICTURES

to select motifs which will be suitable for each area of the work. Small motifs are not difficult to chart out, even if you don't draw well, and you could relate the small motifs to the main subject. For example, if you made a blackwork picture of a car, your little motifs could be made up of repeating designs of car-related items such as steering wheels, funnels, gear sticks, etc. You will need to use fine threads and half-size stitches for very tiny motifs.

It's useful to experiment with motifs on your sampler if you have not worked them before to see their overall effect. You could also use traditional designs such as celtic knots, which are quite fascinating to sew. Filling in an area with motifs is a very relaxing occupation.

95 Motifs with a car theme

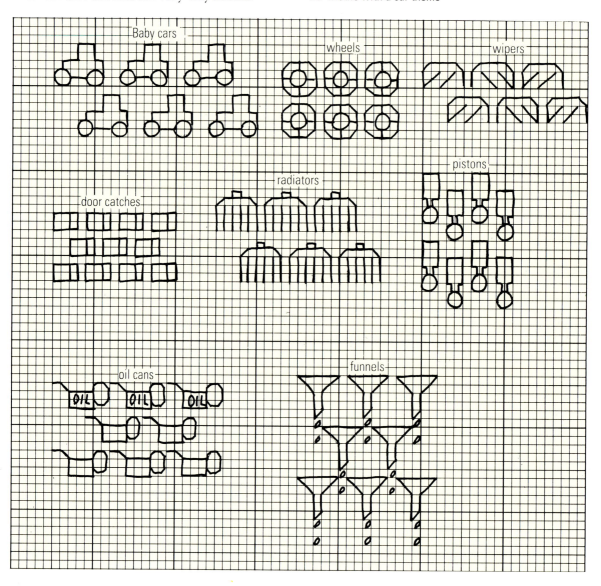

MAKING BLACKWORK PICTURES

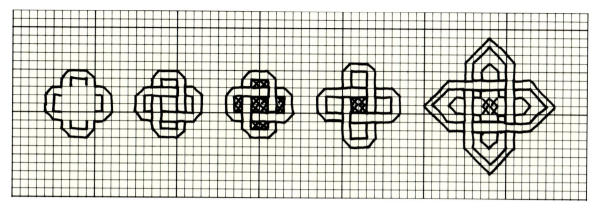

Checking density and 'balance'

96 Developing a celtic knot motif

It is very tempting at the start of a project to push right on and neglect the groundwork. After all, whoever knits the tension squares suggested on knitting patterns?! (Perhaps this is the reason why I have never yet knitted a successful garment, except perhaps a scarf.) But, a word of caution; the *Stitch in Time* sampler has suffered because of my impatience. The motif used to fill the top area is denser than the rest and throws out the whole piece, giving a top-heavy effect. If I had experimented a bit more I could have avoided this problem by swapping over the top and bottom motifs. The second sampler on the same basic theme, *Procrastination is the Thief of Time*, shows a more considered treatment of the blackwork motifs, but impatience is still in evidence; look at the border and the corners. Still, I learn by mistakes and hope you will too.

97 *Stitch in Time* sampler featuring blackwork motifs and pattern darning

98 *Procrastination is the Thief of Time*

105

MAKING BLACKWORK PICTURES

Pattern darning

The *Stitch in time* sampler also illustrates a use of pattern darning. This is extremely simple as only horizontal lines are used and the rows are staggered to achieve different shapes; two sorts of diamond are used in this case.

Working outwards from centre

Once you have done your groundwork, you need to know where to start sewing. I like to find the centre of each particular area and work outwards from there; this will give a balanced appearance. Don't worry if the motif does not finish perfectly at the outline edges; just carry on sewing as normal and stop stitching where it coincides with the outlines. You will see it looks fine when the work is finished.

Outlines

The last task will be finishing off the outlines, if you choose to do so. I prefer to stitch the motifs first and then finish off with the old-fashioned method of a black line around the areas of stitchwork. There are several choices available; you could use back stitch or stem stitch, which would be useful on a curved shape, or you could use a thicker weight thread at this stage. For a really heavy effect you could even lay a thick thread on top and hold it in place with small stitches of finer thread; this is known as couching. A more modern approach is to omit the outlines altogether; use the marking threads during sewing as a guide then remove them when the work is finished to achieve a freer shape.

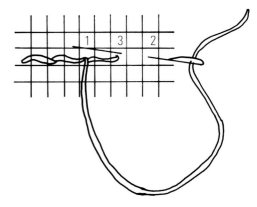

99 Stem stitch.
Work from left to right. Stitch goes forward over four threads, back over two. Up at 1, in at 2, up at 3 – start again

Maps

Maps can be a good design source for blackwork. Two examples are shown on pages 108–9; fig 100 illustrates the layout of Dorothy Banham's farm fields, and opposite it is Sally Gilding's magnificent interpretation of the map of Great Britain. This is worked in varying beiges and browns; blackwork need not necessarily be black.

Presentation

All you have to do now is decide whether or not you need a border for your blackwork picture and finish the work, mounting and framing it in the same way as for the sampler. Then take a step back: the most rewarding part of blackwork embroidery is to stand away from the finished framed picture and see all those different tones you have managed to achieve using only a single colour.

MAKING BLACKWORK PICTURES

Quack Quack by Sally Gilding. Blackwork does not always have to be black. This colour was chosen to complement the decor of a bathroom

MAKING BLACKWORK PICTURES

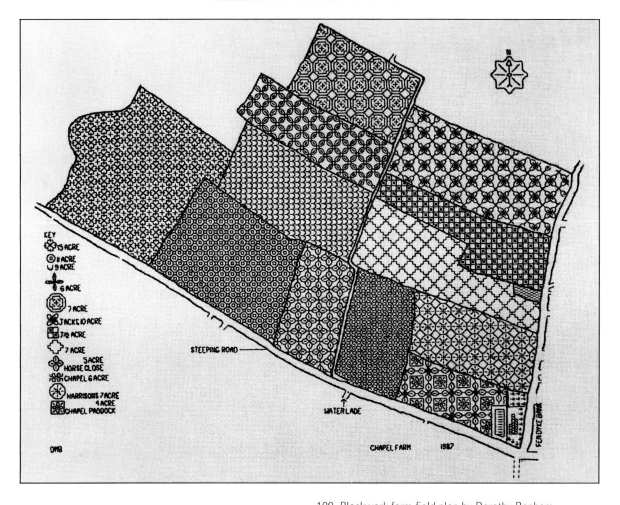

100 Blackwork farm field plan by Dorothy Banham

Work in progress. Sally Gilding is currently working on this magnificent large map of England, Scotland and Wales (size 48 × 74cm/19 × 29in). The design transfer method can be seen at the Western Isles. The map is traced on to tracing paper, then tacked on to fabric and the tracing paper removed, bit by bit, as the blackwork motifs progress. The eventual outline will be a dark back stitch line around the coast. A real heirloom in the making

MAKING BLACKWORK PICTURES

Wide Bargate, Boston. Based on a photograph, loosely interpreted. Metallic threads give sparkle to the windows

MAKING BLACKWORK PICTURES

Home is where the Heart is. Little touches of colour add impact to a mainly monochrome sampler

CHAPTER 6

Samplers for gifts

An individually designed and hand-embroidered sampler makes a truly personalized gift and I have never known one not to be welcome. In fact they can often provoke quite an emotional reaction; many of my students have been puzzled by a tearful response to such a gift (hopefully not tears of disappointment).

Using lettering means that we can celebrate big occasions in our lives; a wedding, a birth, a special anniversary, moving house, etc. It is a pleasure to create a sampler for someone who is special to you and you will see that specialist magazines contain plenty of clever design ideas, particularly for birth and wedding samplers.

My standard celebration sampler layout is shown here on a wedding sampler. I use the gaps at the sides, right and left, to add a very small individually designed motif relating to the recipients. 'PB' is a plumber, so there is a small tap on his side, and 'SC' worked for an organization whose logo was a target, so there is a back-stitch target on her side). You can usually find something about an individual's job or hobby which can translate into a tiny motif.

This standard layout can be adapted for other celebrations. Other motifs can replace the bells and rings, and different words inside the motto border can convert it into a piece for an anniversary celebration or anything else you choose. You can buy gold and silver threads to make colours really appropriate to the celebration.

If you are giving a framed sampler as a gift it is fun to hunt around for just the right quotation or verse so the recipients can feel that it really was made with them in mind. I use the very well-known garden verse in my garden gift sampler for Peg (overleaf), who seems to spend most of the summer in her flowery garden.

Miniature samplers are another idea for gifts or fund-raising craft stalls. The mini-sampler illustrated overleaf is based on a rectangle of only 40 by 55 stitches and is very quick to work. Ready-made photograph frames in this size are also inexpensive, making this a viable gift idea.

Wedding gift sampler for Phil and Sue Brown featuring personalized motifs relevant to the bride and groom

SAMPLERS FOR GIFTS

SAMPLERS FOR GIFTS

Left, a miniature gift sampler to brighten up any small cranny. Opposite, a Silver Wedding celebration. White fabric is used for a better contrast with the silver-grey threads. A metallic thread is combined with stranded cottons for easier handling and a subtle sparkle. Pink and blue threads are used separately for Christian names and combined for the surname. The continuous border is inspired by Roman mosaics. Stitching the border first and adding the centre later is a simpler way to work when the border is complicated like this

Gift sampler featuring a famous garden verse. The flowers at the bottom right are worked in cross stitch and represent aubretia, peony and delphinium. The hanging basket is worked in petit point – very good for fine details, but slow to work

SAMPLERS FOR GIFTS

SAMPLERS FOR GIFTS

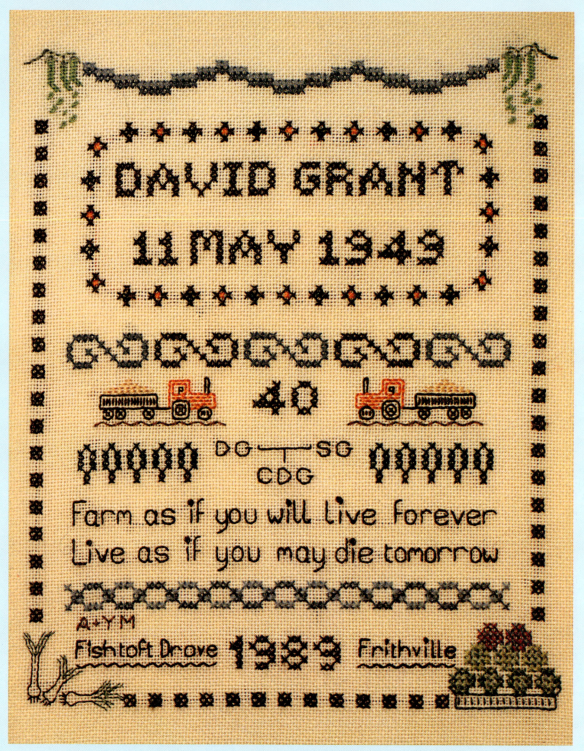

A 40th birthday celebration for a farmer friend featuring his orange tractors and some of his crops

Designs for greetings cards

A gift sampler should be something to be kept and treasured which is why I try to avoid making individual birthday cards. I think it is a shame for a card which is the result of so much time and effort just to be displayed for a week or so and then consigned to a dark cupboard, never again to see the light of day. This is not intended to put you off making greetings cards, but just to stimulate thought about how a greetings card is best presented, and how you can get full value from your work. I like to produce a design and stitch it, then photograph several copies to be mounted in a card.

When you make a card design, try to base it on an outline shape which will be in proportion with the card you will use; the actual size is not so important, as it will be reduced when photographed. It is best not to be too ambitious with designs and to avoid too much detail if you are not experienced; often the simplest ideas are most effective. Look through magazines and old greetings cards to see if there are any ideas which spark off your imagination.

In case you are still a bit nervous about tackling design work, I have included here a design exercise based on a Christmas tree outline. You can see how the original rough sketch is first translated into an outline shape which would be suitable for back stitches. The tree could then be filled with blackwork motifs. The same tree is then further translated into cross stitches; if you work in colour you can then try out garland effects, or blobs of colour to represent tree ornaments. Coloured pencils will be useful here for your experiments. I suggest you then try to chart out a decoration for the top of the tree; an eight-pointed star is a good starting point. Use the same size graph paper as shown for the Christmas trees as the lines will act as a guide.

101 Design charting exercise

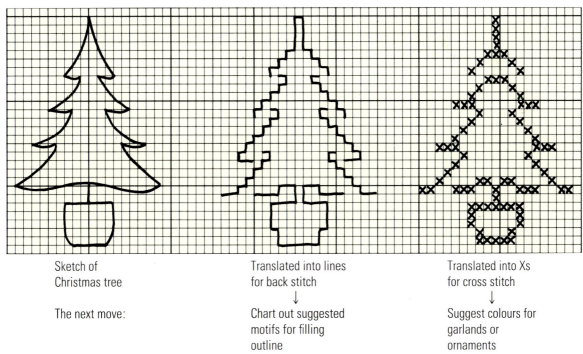

Sketch of
Christmas tree

The next move:

Translated into lines
for back stitch
↓
Chart out suggested
motifs for filling
outline

Translated into Xs
for cross stitch
↓
Suggest colours for
garlands or
ornaments

DESIGNS FOR GREETING CARDS

102 Chart for *Best wishes* card

DESIGNS FOR GREETINGS CARDS

The *Best wishes* card charted here is on a squarish grid to fit into our home-produced three-fold cards. You may wish to try out some new lettering styles; I have included here a new alphabet for you to try, or you can experiment with your own ideas.

To make a card design, follow the same procedure as for making the original sampler. Start by marking out the rectangle or square on graph paper and marking the centre point. Chart out the design on graph paper, using a pencil and eraser, until you are satisfied with your design. Start to think about which colours to use. When you are happy with the design, tack the fabric as before to find and mark the centre point. Then count and tack guide-lines on the fabric to correspond with the chart outline. You can tack extra guide-lines to help you; for example I tacked diagonal lines across the *Best Wishes* fabric so I would know where to change the colours. I was aiming to have diagonal stripes of colour going across the words. When chart and fabric are marked out you are ready to stitch your card design.

103 A different alphabet involving more stitching but still on a very small scale

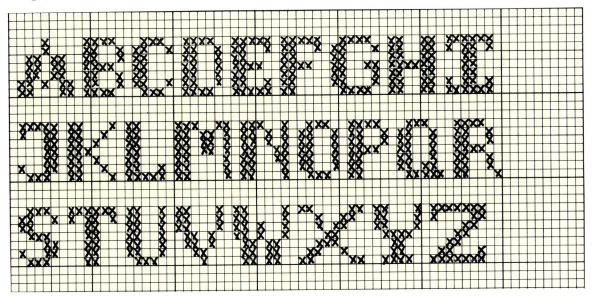

DESIGNS FOR GREETINGS CARDS

Best wishes design for greetings card. Remember to change the design of home-made cards yearly and calculate numbers carefully. Wanting to create the effect of bold colours moving across the lettering in diagonal bands, I tacked guidelines on the fabric when I planned it out so I would know where to make the colour changes

DESIGNS FOR GREETINGS CARDS

A small picture, 9cm (3in) square, with blackwork motifs in different colours

The view through the window is a real departure from the strict discipline of cross stitch, mixing stitches and styles to form an individual picture

A 21st birthday card

A stitched welcome to the new home, 9cm (3in) square

DESIGNS FOR GREETINGS CARDS

Wedding anniversaries. I charted out these numbers to be a suitable size for the centres of small samplers

PRODUCING AND PHOTOGRAPHING A CARD DESIGN

Producing and photographing a card design

We send out an annual Christmas card based on a sampler or canvas work embroidery but it would obviously be out of the question to hand stitch so many. This is the way we go about producing our card.

First of all you need to find a co-operative, competent and experienced photographer. If your photographer has a darkroom, a black and white card is worth thinking about. Blackwork embroidery and back-stitch designs lend themselves very nicely to being photographed in monochrome and your photographer will be able to home produce all the prints. Otherwise, you can make a colour design and have colour prints processed professionally.

In September, or thereabouts, I chart out and sew a design. (You could of course leave this until early December if you like to panic or have no relatives in Australia). This is then finished and laced on to board in the same way as described for finishing off the sampler. It is then photographed; a few experimental shots at the end of the holiday snaps film will soon show which was the best camera setting, lighting arrangement and other details.

Hints and advice for photographing embroideries

If you are photographing any number of a design for a greetings card, take a few shots, noting down details of exposure, lighting, distance between camera and sampler, your set-up, and so on. Then you can see from the prints which arrangement works best, and use the formula when taking the photographs in large numbers. This could avoid expensive mistakes.

Christmas greetings card design featuring multi-coloured paper chains, lettering and Christmas ideas

PRODUCING AND PHOTOGRAPHING A CARD DESIGN

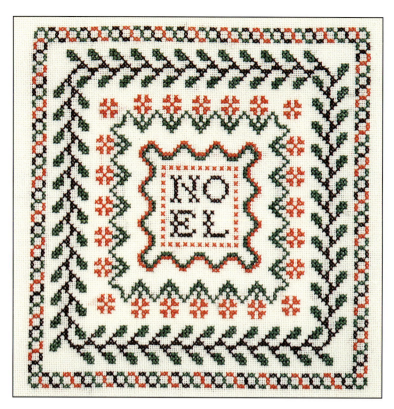

Noel. Christmas card design worked as an experiment in using borders radiating out from the centre. The chart is planned using a 45 degree triangle up from the centre. The other three quarters are repeat images of the first triangle, with the work turned. For this to work accurately, the centre lettering has to fit inside a square

Use a 35 mm SLR camera with a 50 mm lens, or something even better like a medium format camera if you are lucky enough to have one. To use natural light you will probably need to work outside. Choose a suitably overcast day with good steady light, and beware of shadows from other objects. To use artificial light, experiment with table lamps or spotlights until you achieve a pleasing effect. Use a blue 80B filter with artificial light to avoid yellowing of the image if photographing in colour.

Check and double check carefully through the viewfinder before releasing the shutter. The camera needs to be held square-on to the embroidery to avoid distortion of the image. Rig up a tripod or something firm to hold the camera completely steady. Remember you will be taking several shots; a remote-control shutter release will prevent camera shake.

Samplers are best photographed before framing, or inside the frame but without the glass. Glass over the work can cause problems with unwelcome reflections and highlights. If glass cannot be removed, use a polarising filter to cut reflections to a minimum.

For greetings cards we have found, to date, that it is more economical to take thirty-six separate, identical, shots of the design and then to have the film developed and printed with a spare set of prints. This seems to work out more cheaply than taking one shot and having reprints made, but do check locally; a lot will depend on how many cards you wish to produce.

PRODUCING AND PHOTOGRAPHING A CARD DESIGN

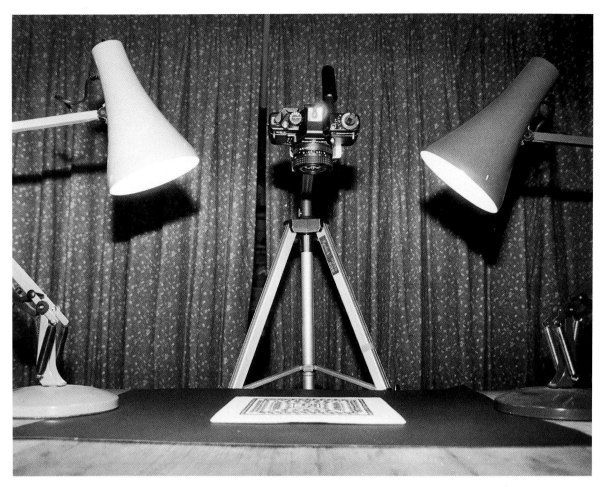

104 Home set-up for photographing samplers and greetings card designs

Making cards

As well as the photographs, you will need some cards with a hole cut out which fits round the photograph. You can buy greetings cards specially made for displaying photographs or craft work. An alternative is to obtain some plain card, or thick paper, and cut the hole yourself. This can be a tricky job if you are not too handy with a craft knife, so you could research around your local printers. Some printers have machines which will make fold lines in the card for you and also stamp out a hole. They might also print your greetings inside the card which will save a lot of handwriting.

If all this seems too complicated, you could always opt to glue the photograph to the front of the card, but this does not give such a professional looking finish as when the photograph is mounted under the card.

Whichever display method you choose, it takes only a couple of evenings of folding and gluing (while discussing the Christmas card list), and the cards are ready to send out. It is very flattering to think that friends are making collections of one's home-made greetings cards, but it certainly puts the pressure on to try to think of a new and better design each year!

PRODUCING AND PHOTOGRAPHING A CARD DESIGN

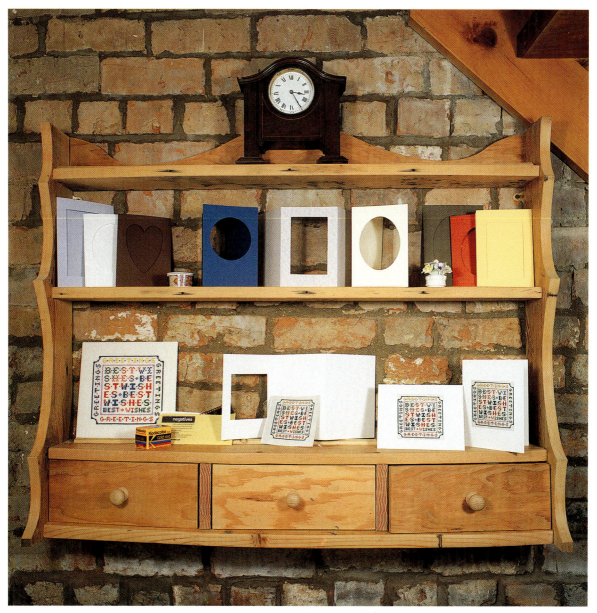

Making a greetings card. The top shelf shows a variety of shapes and colours available in blank cards. The lower shelf follows the card-producing process from left to right. Cut square aperture cards can be used either sideways or upright

FURTHER READING

I hope that this book has started an interest which will give you pleasure for many years. I include here a list of books which will provide valuable further reading and ideas.

CIRKER, Blanche, *Needlework Alphabets and Designs*, Dover, 1975

COLBY, Averil, *Samplers*, Batsford, 1964, 1987

DON, Sarah, *Traditional Samplers*, David & Charles, 1986

EATON, Jan & MUNDLE, Liz, *The Cross Stitch and Sampler Book*, Apple Press, 1985

GEDDES, Elisabeth & MCNEILL, Moyra, *Blackwork Embroidery*, Dover, 1976

MODES & TRAVAUX, *A Sampler of Alphabets*, Sterling Publishing, 1987

PASCOE Margaret, *Blackwork Embroidery: Design & Technique*, Batsford, 1986

SUPPLIERS

The following suppliers offer a mail order service for fabric and threads. The Lanarte fabric is a 27-thread cream evenweave (ref. No. 47197):

Spinning Jenny
Bradley
Keighley
W. Yorkshire BD20 9DD (Lanarte distributors in Great Britain)

Mace & Nairn
89 Crane Street
Salisbury
Wilts SP1 2PY

Campden Needlecraft Centre
High Street
Chipping Campden
Glos

Voirrey Embroidery Centre
Brimstage Hall
Brimstage
Wirral L63 63A

Christine Riley
53 Barclay Street
Stonehaven
Kincardineshire AB3 2AR

Fencraft
45 Wormgate-by-the-Stump
Boston
Lincs PR21 6NS (My local supplier)

Blank cards for display craft work are supplied by mail order from:

Impress Cards
Slough Farm
Westhall
Halesworth
Suffolk IP19 8RN

INDEX

Adjustments 33, 63, 67–70
Aida fabric 11, 33
Alphabets 10–11, 21–2, 28, 41–2, 44, 120

Back stitch 15, 40
Band samplers 29
Blackwork 91
   motifs 96–9, 104–5
   planning a design 102
   threads 93
Borders, continuous 62–70
   uncounted 70–3

Cards, greetings 118–26
Centre
   lines 17
   point 18
Centring
   alphabet and patterns 21, 33
   a motif 57
Chart 10, 17, 21, 33
Charting exercise 21, 118
Colour 13–14, 27, 59, 73
Couching 106
Counted thread embroidery 11, 14
Cross stitch 14
Cut and paste 56

Decorative motifs 29, 33
Design equipment 11
Design transfer methods 103
Double running stitch 95

Enlarging/reducing 49–51
Equipment 11
Evenweave 11

Fabric 11, 13, 17
Finishing and mounting 74–8

Four-sided stitch 58
Frames
   presentation 73
   sewing 13
Fraying edges 17
French knots 59

Geometric shapes 95
Gifts and greetings 112
Graph paper 11, 14, 17

Half stitches 40–1
Hemming 17
Hoops 13, 24
Houses 45–7

Initials 21–2

Kits 10
Knots, Celtic 105

Lanarte 11
Layout 21, 35
Letters, stitching 28
Lighting 22

Magnifier 11, 22
Maps 106
Materials 11
Mistakes 8, 26
Mitring corners 17, 77
Motifs 29
   pictorial 51–57, 60
   spot 56
   blackwork 93, 95–8, 104–5
Mottoes 10, 35–8

Needles 13, 25
Numbers 21–2, 41–2

Pattern 30–1, 33

Pattern darning 106
Petit point 58
Photographing work 123–4
Photographs, working from 47–8
Pictorial motifs 51–7, 60
Posture 22
Preparing fabric 17
Presentation 73
Pricking the ground 58

Rectangle 17, 19
Roman numerals 44

Sewing equipment 11–13
Sewing techniques 22, 25
Spot motifs 56
Squaring up 49–51
Starting and finishing 25–6
Stem stitch 106
Stitches
   back stitch 15, 40
   cross stitch 15
   double running 95
   four sided 58
   french knots 59
   half 40–1
   petit point 58
   stem 106
Stranded cotton 13–4, 25

Tacking threads 18–19
Techniques 22, 25
Threads 13
   for blackwork 94
Tracing designs 48

Washing samplers 74–5
Working method 14–16